Great Leaders Make Great Parents

Have you ever experienced a defining moment in your life? I mean, one of those moments which was so profound and memorable that you're constantly reminded of it for the rest of your life? One of my moments came on March 24, 1992. My wife Colleen and I were in the parking lot at Rochester Memorial Hospital. Technically it was Spring, but this was Rochester, New York. It was a balmy 23 degrees with high winds blowing onshore from Lake Ontario. Wrapped up and buckled in the second row of our Ford Taurus station wagon was the newest addition to our family, Emily Elizabeth. A mere 48 hours ago it was just Colleen and I driving to the hospital. Now there was a 7 lb 4 oz baby girl coming home with us equipped with no user guide or instruction manual. I remember looking into her big brown eyes. She was so helpless and dependent! On the drive home, I was overwhelmed with a stream of random thoughts and emotions. On one hand, I felt honored, privileged and proud to be a new Dad. On the other hand, I was experiencing serious self-doubt about my maturity and ability to be a parent. To be honest, I could barely take care of myself, let alone take responsibility for this helpless newborn. Was I even qualified for such a monumental task? What if I screwed it up?

Fast forward to September 22, 1999. It was another one of those defining moments. I was sitting in the CEO's office at our corporate headquarters in Salem, New Jersey. I was offered a promotion to the position of Vice President of Sales. Keep in mind that at that point in my career, I had never managed other people before. To be honest, I could barely manage myself, let alone an entire sales organization. Some very familiar thoughts and emotions gripped me. Though I felt honored and privileged that the CEO placed his trust in me to lead the sales organization, I was questioning my own maturity and ability to lead others in the workplace. Effectively leading all of these people would be a huge responsibility, and I was feeling the weight of it. They would be looking to me for direction and support. Most of them had families of their own which placed an even greater burden of responsibility on my shoulders. Once again self-doubt crept in. Was I even qualified for this? I really didn't think so. What if I screwed it up?

My reactions and concerns about becoming a first-time parent and a leader to others in the workplace were obviously quite similar.

I didn't realize until later in life, however, that there are even more similarities between **being** *a parent and a leader than most folks realize. There is a set of underlying values, traits and beliefs, which are equally relevant and similar in fulfilling the responsibilities of both a parent and a leader in the workplace. That's why I believe that great leaders make great parents and great parents make great leaders.*

Let's start with two underlying assumptions about parenting and leading others in the workplace. The first is that *fulfilling both roles are much more of a journey than a destination.* A destination implies an eventual finish line. There is no finish line as a parent or a leader. You don't wake up one morning and say, "My work is done here. There is nothing more for me to do or improve upon." If you think for a minute that "your work is done," meaning that you have achieved mastery and excellence as a leader and a parent and that there is nothing more to do, then you are seriously deluding yourself. Both parenting and leading are far more complex than mastering a simple task. Let me give you an example. Properly folding a fitted bed sheet is considered a task. At some point, you can be taught the proper way to fold a fitted sheet. (This may be a poor example. I've been instructed repeatedly on this matter and I'm not even close to getting it right.) Anyway, sooner or later, the average Joe can probably master this task and might even say, "Tah-dah. I got this!" Now as far as being a parent, you might say "I got this" for a singular parenting task, such as effectively teaching your daughter to tell time.

But parenting or leading others, as a discipline, is an endless journey

comprised of thousands of tasks, behaviors and decision points, all of which are heavily influenced by underlying values, traits and beliefs.

Kind of tough to say "Tah-dah, I got this" for all of it.

The second underlying assumption I'm making is that **parenting and leading others is more of an Art than a Science.** It is very simple: both roles require constant interaction with other human beings. It is far less complex and frustrating to manage a project, process or piece of machinery than it is to manage people. Scientific formulas work much better on things than they do on people. Whether they are adults or children, people are unpredictable. They are notoriously difficult to understand in terms of why and how they behave and make decisions. It's often nearly impossible to influence or control them, and it can be mind-boggling trying to figure out what truly motivates them. Not to mention, parenting and leading others can be extremely exhausting work, especially if you are more of an introvert than an extrovert. Direct reports and children will suck the life out of you. It is so important to find ways to recharge your battery, particularly if you tend to be more of an introvert, as I am by nature. As a parent and workplace leader, I was often exhausted by the end of the day. For me, landscaping was my escape. The beauty of landscaping is in carrying out simple, well defined tasks and achieving tangible results. It's one of life's simple pleasures. The best part of this relaxing pastime is that the grass and bushes can't talk back to you and complain about the quality of your work.

Although I believe that parenting and leading others is more of an Art than a Science, I do believe that there are some relevant behavioral science principles which apply to both. This reminds me of a funny story. I graduated from the University of Rochester in 1981 with a degree in Psychology. At the time, I can remember a large concentration of students focused on pre-law, pre-med, engineering and other Hard Science curriculums. I also remember taking a beating from my friends and classmates about my choice in Majors. One time I was sitting in a bathroom stall and saw a message on the wall with an arrow pointing to a roll of toilet paper. The message read, "Psychology degrees...take one." The underlying message was that Psychology as a Major was neither marketable nor relevant in the real world. I will admit that I took this message to heart. Interestingly enough, as it turned out, I have found my degree in Psychology to be quite useful. Behavioral Modification, Conditioning, Motivation Theory and Reward Structures all have relevant applications for parenting and leading others, which I will periodically refer to throughout the book.

Since this book is entitled "8 Humble Lessons Learned as a Leader and a Parent," I'd like to talk briefly about humility. It is defined as "a modest view of one's own importance." I think this is a very healthy trait to possess, particularly as a parent or a leader of others. A friend of mine once told me that it is ok to take your work seriously but never to take yourself too seriously. I think there is a lot of truth to that. I have a Master's Degree in Organizational Development. I've completed continuing education classes in Sales, Human Resources and Leadership from Wharton, Cornell, The University of Chicago and countless other institutions. I have 28 years of experience as a parent and over 20 years of experience leading others in the workplace. And guess what? Despite my experiences and training, I can honestly say that I've made just about every mistake in the book as a leader and a parent. In fact, I have had moments when I have been completely overwhelmed by my own incompetence. I can't begin to tell you the number of times that I have made poor decisions or the number of times I have misread or misunderstood others. It is very humbling.

I also think that great life lessons are born from humility. Any time I have become consciously aware of my own incompetence, it has created discomfort and humiliation. Discomfort and humiliation, albeit very painful feelings, serve as motivation which fuels learning and positive change.

It happens a lot as a parent and a leader. I have another funny story regarding the topic of humility. I took up the game of golf at the age of forty. I had recently been promoted into a sales leadership position and thought that golf would be a great way to help build relationships with customers. In addition, I worked for a privately held, family owned business. The chairman of the board and owner was Scottish. His father was Scottish. His grandfather was Scottish. His great grandfather was Scottish. You get the picture. The Scots invented golf and are very proud of it. Needless to say, I was feeling a little pressure to step up. One of my first company golf outings was at Pebble Beach. For those of you unfamiliar with golf, Pebble Beach sits on the Pacific Ocean in California and is widely considered the mecca of all golf courses. I was looking forward to the trip. I was always a pretty good athlete and thought to myself, "How difficult could it be to smack a stationary ball with a stick?" Well, I posted a score of about 150 at Pebble Beach and I cheated on a few holes to boot. Pretty good score for bowling. Not so good for golf. Being an extremely competitive person, I cannot describe to you the frustration and humiliation I felt. Before I took up the game of golf, I was completely unaware of how incompetent I was. I finally understood the true meaning of the popular expression, "Ignorance is bliss." Parenting and leading others, just like playing golf, can be very frustrating and humiliating, particularly when you become consciously aware that you are not nearly as good as you think. But again, without being consciously aware of our shortcomings, there is no discomfort. And with no pain, there is no motivation to change. For what it's worth, despite years of practice, on a really good day, I've never been more than a mediocre golfer. I hit enough bad shots to keep me humble and just enough good shots to keep me hopeful. Just before I retired, I golfed with a customer who said to me, "You don't have to throw the game just to make me look good." This is too funny. I told him, "Do you really think I'm deliberately hitting the ball in the woods, in the sand traps, in the water and on to the wrong fairways for the sake of good customer relations? Well you don't know me very well. Trust me. If I could,

I'd wipe the floors with you on the golf course!"

In summary, it is my belief that parenting and leading others is a journey as opposed to a destination. Both are more of an Art than a Science. Both can be very humiliating. Nevertheless, both can be extremely rewarding.

In my experience, nothing has been more satisfying than to observe my direct reports and my children grow in self-confidence and become competent and independent decision makers.

Knowing that in some small way, I contributed to their growth has been a great source of pride for me.

Speaking of humility, I do not claim to be an expert in parenting or leading others. In fact,

I have a hard time believing *anyone* is truly an expert at parenting or leading. I have had a few shining moments. I have also had many moments when I would consider myself average. In general, I think I've been a pretty good leader and parent (although the truth would have to come from my direct reports and children). As far as I'm concerned, being "pretty good" isn't all that bad given the never-ending challenges and complexities inherent in leading and parenting. I was recently vacationing in the Pocono Mountains and I saw a guy wearing an awesome t-shirt. It read: "World's most OK-est Dad." The grammar is bad, but the message is right on Ok is pretty damn good when you consider that there are hundreds of thousands of leaders and parents out there that are far less than ok. By the way, regarding the title of the book, the only reason I referenced the word "great" is that I thought it might sell more books. It was a shameless marketing ploy. Being a truly "great" leader and parent is awfully difficult to achieve for most mortals.

Through this never-ending journey, and through a humiliating process of failing forward, I've learned several lessons which have served me well as a parent and leader of others in the workplace. The following chapters will outline these lessons learned. I'll use very specific examples, based upon my own experiences, to describe these learnings. I've added a touch of humor along the way as well in the hope of making this experience both informative and entertaining.

Lesson One:

Values, Traits and Beliefs Influence Behavior

Ok. I'm coming right out of the gate a little heavy on Psychology 101. Please bear with me for a moment because this is really important.

One of my greatest life lessons is that most everything I have done, everything I have said and every decision I have made, as a parent and a leader of others, has been heavily influenced by a bunch of stuff that I'm not even consciously aware of.

This probably sounds strange to you, but it's very true. I'm going out on a limb here by saying that you are probably no different than me and that **your** actions and behaviors are also heavily influenced by this stuff as well. I'd like to explain this by using an analogy. If you think about an iceberg, the vast majority of it remains hidden beneath the surface of the water. Only a very small fraction of it is visible above the water. Likewise, we all have a number of values, traits and beliefs which are hidden from view and are operating beneath the surface. This "stuff" may be hidden from view but is extremely powerful and influential and manifests itself daily through our actions and behaviors. These actions and behaviors represent the tiny portion of the iceberg which is above the surface of the water and can readily be seen by the human eye. I have recently been doing a lot of soul searching and I've been fascinated by the extent to which my actions and behaviors are controlled and influenced by my values, traits and beliefs. I'd like to start by defining and explaining these terms and using specific examples of how they influence our behaviors and actions as parents and leaders:

Values

a person's principles or standards of behavior; one's judgement of what is important in life

We all have certain underlying standards of behavior and things in life which we truly value, although we may not be consciously aware of what they are. Here are two examples of commonly communicated values: "family is really important to me" and "staying healthy and physically fit is very important in my life." Sometimes there is a disconnect between a stated value and an observed behavior. For example, you might have a friend who says, "my family is everything to me" yet you've observed that they never spend time with their children or that they have been unfaithful to their spouse. In this case, there is clearly an inconsistency between what this person **says** and what they actually **do**. But make no mistake about it, **what this person does is very consistent with what they truly value.** Do you see the difference? By the way, I don't think this sort of thing is all that uncommon. In fact, most people are guilty of this from time to time. How often have you listened to others talk about what they value only to observe that their actions and behaviors are almost the exact opposite of the words they are using? In my mind, this is the very definition of hypocrisy. On occasion, I have been guilty of being hypocritical but I'm pretty certain that I'm a saint as compared to many other people around me.

Trait

a distinguishing quality or characteristic, typically one belonging to a person

Just like values, we all have a number of traits that distinguish us from others. Here are some examples of traits people might possess: generosity, integrity, self-control and kindness. Values and traits are deeply imbedded in who we are as human beings. Both develop very early in life through significant life experiences. Arguably we are all genetically predisposed to certain values and traits. In other words, some values and traits are "hard wired" regardless of our experiences while growing up.

Beliefs

something one accepts as true or real; a firmly held conviction

Just like values and traits, we all have things that we strongly believe in. For example, I have a belief that the New York Giants football team will once again rise from the ashes and return to greatness by winning another Super Bowl within the next three years. My belief is neither right nor wrong. It is neither good nor bad. ***It simply is what it is.*** By the way, I have friends and neighbors who would argue vehemently about this. Keep in mind that I live just outside of Philadelphia. There is no love lost between the Philadelphia Eagles and the New York Giants. In fact, there is no love lost between Eagles fans and any human being that stands in their way. I think that Eagles fans would throw mustard at Mother Theresa if she was wearing the opposing team's jersey at Lincoln Financial Stadium. By the way, **beliefs, traits and values, once formed, do not change very easily**. I realize that this sounds very pessimistic, but it is so true. I have countless personal examples of failed attempts to coach and train others to do things differently. The problem was that the things I wanted others to do differently were very inconsistent with their underlying values, traits and beliefs. Guess what? Behavioral change never happened despite all of the time and energy spent on coaching and training. I'll talk more about this later in the book.

Behavior

the way in which one acts or conducts oneself, especially towards others

Let's discuss the term, Behavior. Simply put, it refers to **what you do or how** you act. As discussed in the iceberg analogy, behaviors and actions are those things that are above the surface of the water. They are the things that we can physically observe. They are the things that are very strongly influenced by values, traits and beliefs. By the way, as the father of three beautiful daughters, I have a personal **belief** that their boyfriends should always feel intimidated by me. I'm not proud of this but I can't help myself. This is a case where my beliefs affect my actions and behaviors. It has also been my hope that my beliefs affect my **daughters' boyfriends'** actions and behaviors as well, if you know what I mean.

So enough with the psychobabble. What does any of this have to do with either parenting or leading others in the workplace?

We all have a number of personal Values, Traits and Beliefs that serve as a powerful standard for how we behave, or act, every single hour of every single day of our lives. Our Values, Traits and Beliefs influence every move we make as parents and leaders of others in the workplace.

As I said earlier, this has been one of the greatest lessons learned in my life as a parent and a leader. Well not exactly. I lied about the greatest lesson thing. Truth be told, the greatest lesson I've learned in life is that my wife is always right and I'm always wrong. This belief has kept my wife and I happily married for over 30 years. In fact, I have had mornings when I wake up, turn to my wife and say, "Honey, I'm sorry." Then she will say, 'What are you sorry about?" Then I say, "Does it really matter? Whatever goes wrong today is my fault. If the power goes out in our neighborhood, it's on me. If we get hit by a tsunami, I'm truly sorry and I'll try to do better next time." Anyway, I'm digressing again so let's get back on track. Over the last year or so, I have tried to become consciously aware of my own Values, Traits and Beliefs, particularly as they relate to parenting and leading others. I'd like to discuss some of these and the influence they have had on my actions and behavior as a parent and leader. My hope is that this will stimulate you to take a step back and think about the many ways in which your own Values, Traits and Beliefs have influenced **your** behaviors and actions:

"I believe *that people are generally trustworthy until proven otherwise*"

This is an underlying belief I have had for as long as I could remember. It has played a large role in influencing my behavior as both a parent and leader of others. I've been accused on more than one occasion of being naïve and too trusting. I'll admit that there is some truth to this. There are times when direct reports and my own children have taken advantage of me. It's kind of ironic that I'm very trusting of others because I was born and raised in New York City. As New Yorkers, we are often accused of not even trusting our own mothers. Anyway, let me give you an example of how my belief about trusting others has influenced my behavior as a parent. My wife and I have three daughters. We have never kept hidden cameras inside or outside of our house to monitor their activities. We have never tracked their whereabouts on smart phones.

We never jumped in the car and secretly followed them to be sure they were going where they said they were going. We never did these things because we trusted them to be truthful with us and do the right thing. And unless they gave us a valid reason why they **shouldn't** be trusted we didn't spend much time trying to secretly catch them betraying the trust we placed in them.

There are two other reasons why we didn't secretly monitor our kid's activities. First, my wife and I believed that our kids were creative and resourceful enough to "game the system" despite any efforts to control and monitor their actions. Second, we were uncomfortable with the message that we would be sending to our daughters if we secretly monitored their whereabouts. And that message is, "you are not to be trusted." We never thought that would build their confidence and self-esteem.

In fact, I am thoroughly convinced that when others are trusted, and they are fully aware that they are being trusted, that really good things happen.

First, they are honored that they are being trusted and become determined not to let you down. Second, their confidence and competence is bolstered. I have a good example of this. It was 2006 and our oldest daughter was 14 years old. She just came back from a visit with our neighbors, the Iannucci's. She was super excited. She told us that the Iannucci's allowed her to hold their daughter who had been born just 48 hours ago. You should have seen the look in her eyes. She couldn't believe that our neighbors placed their trust in her to hold their baby girl. Our daughter was so honored. She routinely came home from school and spent time with our neighbor's daughter several times a week. Interestingly enough, our daughter is now a Pediatrician and I can't help but believe that her choice was influenced in some small way by this random act of trust that our neighbors placed in her. Some of you would consider our approach to raising our children to be quite naïve and irresponsible. I can appreciate that, especially if your underlying belief is that children should not be trusted until they prove that they are trustworthy. It really doesn't matter if we agree on this or not. ***My point is that beliefs and values heavily influence our behaviors.*** Now, all of that being said, ***if*** our daughters had ever taken advantage of the trust that we placed in them, or if we felt that their safety and security were at risk, then we would have taken a much more controlling approach to raising them. Fortunately, we were never faced with such a dilemma.

My belief about trusting others has also influenced my behaviors and actions as a leader. For example, in my role as Vice

President of Sales, I never focused much attention on monitoring and analyzing my staff's Travel and Expense reports and budgets. Sure, I would spot check their expense reports, but I never obsessed over them. First of all, I expected my staff to do the right thing and, more importantly, I trusted them to act responsibly regarding company spending. If they were deliberately cheating the system, then I made a really bad decision by hiring them in the first place. My time was far better spent helping them to achieve their sales goals than it was tormenting them as to why they spent an additional $50 flying directly to Philadelphia International Airport as opposed to laying over in Atlanta to save a few bucks. Also, I wanted them to know that it was far more valuable for them to generate millions of dollars in profitable sales than it was to cut a few dollars in travel and entertainment expenses. If my internal belief was that people are not to be trusted until they prove to be trustworthy, my actions and behaviors would have been much different. I probably would have spent a lot more time diving into spending reports to be sure my staff was complying with company guidelines. To reiterate, I'm not saying that my management approach was the right approach. I'm saying that *my personal belief that people are trustworthy until proven otherwise had a tremendous influence on how I behaved as a leader.*

Here's another belief that is deeply embedded inside of me:

"I believe that people want to succeed and do the right thing"

This belief has heavily influenced my approach to dealing with issues of non-performance as both a parent and a leader of others. Have you ever wondered why people do not do what they are supposed to do? Is it because they simply do not care? Is it because people are inherently lazy? Earlier in my career, I read a book entitled, Coaching for Improved Performance, written by Ferdinand Fournies. It was one of the best books I have ever read on the topics of coaching and performance management. Ferdinand thoroughly explored this question of why people do not do what they are supposed to do. I can't help but believe that he shared my fundamental belief that people really want to succeed and do the right thing. In a nutshell, Ferdinand was saying that when people don't do what they are supposed to, don't just write them off as being lazy. Do a little investigative work to really understand what is causing non-performance. I have personally practiced this for many years as a parent and leader. For example, when others don't do what they are supposed to do, I ask myself the following questions:

- **Were they ever explicitly told what was expected of them?**

It has been my experience that most times others will perform just fine once they know what is truly expected of them. I recently had a conversation with a drug and alcohol counselor. He told me that an alarming number of his teenage patients claimed that their parents never explicitly told them that drugs were forbidden in their households. This blew me away. I suppose that sometimes we overlook the obvious as parents.

- **Were they ever trained properly?**

It is possible that others know what is expected of them, but they simply do not know **how** to do it. It could be that they are embarrassed to admit that they do not know how to perform a given task. That's where a good leader or parent can step in to provide training and coaching.

- **Do they get punished for good performance?**

  In other words, are people somehow punished for doing what they are supposed to do? This sounds crazy, doesn't it? Yet I have an example of this. As a leader, I have been guilty of piling up the workload on direct reports that can handle it. At some point I've overloaded them and, ironically, punished them for doing a good job.

- **Do they get rewarded for non-performance?**

Your daughter Rachel does such a terrible job of emptying the dishwasher that you turn the responsibility over to your son, Kyle, who does a much better job of it. You've just rewarded Rachel for non-performance by letting her off the hook. (in addition to pissing off Kyle)

- **Are there obstacles beyond their control?**

As a sales leader, for example, when sales representatives fail to achieve sales growth targets, it is easy to assume that they don't have what it takes to get the job done. Sometimes, however, there are legitimate obstacles which are beyond their control which prevent them from hitting sales targets. For example, the market could be soft or the products they are selling are not competitively priced. Although these obstacles can be very difficult to eliminate, a good leader will at least acknowledge them and work as hard as possible to mitigate them.

Since Beliefs, Traits and Values influence behaviors, if my internal belief was that people are inherently lazy and not motivated to succeed, I would not have wasted time addressing the issues above when dealing with non-performance. I would not have bothered ensuring that my direct reports clearly understood what was being asked of them. I would not have gone out of my way providing coaching and training for them, or removing obstacles that prevented them from doing their jobs properly. I'd probably be quicker to pull the trigger and terminate their employment. By the way, regarding the topic of termination, I'm obviously referring to employees in the workplace and not our own children. We can't terminate our children, although we have all had moments when that would have been tempting. This would have made for a very funny Saturday Night Live skit:

"Ben, thanks for taking this meeting with your Mom and me. We know how busy your schedule is. Let's just cut to the chase. Your performance as our son has been disappointing, to say the least. Despite our repeated efforts to coach and train you, you're just not getting it done. We are going to have to cut you loose. The good news is that we would be happy to serve as a reference for you if the opportunity presents itself. We will also throw in health insurance coverage through the end of the year. You might want to try the Johnson's down the street. They have two daughters and might be interested in picking up a son. Well, we wish you the best and please don't take this personally, it's purely a business decision."

I have discussed two deeply seated beliefs which have had a very strong influence on my behaviors and actions as a parent. Now I'd like to discuss a personal trait of mine which has also influenced my behaviors and actions. The trait I'm referring to is Selfishness. It has been the bane of my existence as a parent and leader for many years:

"I am a selfish human being"

Talk about an underlying trait that has profoundly influenced my behavior as a parent and leader. Wow! What makes this so humiliating is that each and every day I am consciously aware of my selfishness, but it is a deeply rooted trait and not easily changed. Don't get me wrong, I've gotten better as both a parent and a leader, but I still have a lot of work in front of me. My wife, on the other hand is the most unselfish human being I've ever known. I have learned an awful lot from her, as a parent, by witnessing her behavior with our children. I'll be exploring this topic of selfishness in greater detail in the next chapter.

In summary, whether inherited at birth or acquired through early life experiences, we all have deeply imbedded values, traits and beliefs that have a tremendous influence on our behaviors and actions as parents and leaders. Through self-awareness, we can recognize our values, traits and beliefs and the powerful role they play in influencing our actions and behaviors. We can even alter our values, traits and beliefs, in order to become better leaders and parents, although this is not easily accomplished.

Lesson Two

Capitalize on Other's Strengths

An undeniable truth is that all human beings possess inherent strengths and weaknesses. This truth applies equally to the children we are parenting and the direct reports we are leading in the workplace. The only exception to the rule was a gentleman I interviewed for a sales position about 10 years ago. During the interview, I asked him to tell me about a personal weakness that he was aware of and trying to improve. After pondering this at length, he looked me in the eye and said, "Gosh, quite frankly, I really don't have any weaknesses." I was dumbfounded by this comment. I was tempted to respond by saying, "For starters, self-awareness would have to be up there as far as your many weaknesses." Needless to say, this guy wasn't invited back for additional interviews. Honestly, what are these people thinking? Even if you really didn't believe you had any weaknesses, would you be stupid enough to state it so bluntly during a job interview?

One of my epic failures as a parent and a leader, especially in my earlier years, was spending way too much time and energy focused on trying to correct others' weaknesses, instead of capitalizing on their strengths.

This learning has come at a personal price for me. As a parent and leader for nearly 30 years, it would not surprise me one bit if I actually spent more than one full year of my life dedicated to this. Sadly, despite all of this time and energy expended, I have had a poor track record of influencing others to convert their weaknesses into strengths.

I want to draw a distinction between correcting others' mistakes, as opposed to correcting their weaknesses. As an example, suppose your third grader scores a "C" on a math exam because he messed up on a few questions dealing with fractions. Up until this point, your son has been pretty good with fractions. As a parent, you either personally help him work through the mistakes or you put it back on him to discover for himself why he incorrectly multiplied a few fractions. In either case, you do what any good parent would: help your son to correct his mistakes and learn from them. Let's say that you also have a daughter who happens to struggle with attention to detail. This is manifested often and in many ways. You're not sure why she lacks attention to detail. Is it the way her brain works? Is it a chemical thing? Is it something she inherited from her dad? (In my case, absolutely.) In this context, lack of attention to detail is less likely to be a series of mistakes made but rather, a character flaw or weakness in your daughter. One option is to dedicate an inordinate amount of time and energy in turning this weakness into a strength. In other words, try to help your daughter to become detail oriented in everything she does. In my opinion, this is not a very good or efficient use of time. Sure, you might help her with some strategies to help her become a little more detail oriented. However, as I have been saying, it is extremely difficult to change others' traits or personal character. On top of that, you'll probably frustrate your daughter by trying to change her into something she is not. The other option which, in my opinion, is much more productive and invigorating is to exploit and capitalize on any one of several inherent strengths that your daughter does possess and run with it. It is certainly understandable to want to turn your kids' weaknesses into strengths, but I'm reminded of a great quote that sums it up nicely:

"Love and embrace the children that you have and not the children that you had hoped for."

By the way, another revelation of mine has been that all of my children's strengths have been inherited from their mom. On the other hand, all of their weaknesses have been inherited from their dad. It's funny how that works, isn't it?

At the end of the day there is only a finite amount of time and energy available as a leader and a parent. It is far more productive and efficient to use that time and energy to embrace, direct and encourage others' strengths than it is to focus on trying to correct their weaknesses.

Capitalizing on Your Children's Strengths

As a parent, one of the greatest gifts you can give your children is to help them recognize, embrace and capitalize on their inherent strengths. Kids today are under a tremendous amount of pressure to succeed. Competition for really good jobs has accelerated. As crazy as it seems, the marketplace has truly become global. There's a bunch of kids taking SAT preparatory courses as early as the 5th grade. The workload on these kids has intensified. Quite frankly, I never experienced any of this growing up. We did a little homework, but we certainly didn't study until midnight. It's easy for kids to pressure themselves into taking a bunch of classes and majoring in something that is highly marketable, but in no way plays to their strengths. Huge mistake!

As a parent, I always felt that it was important to take notice of my daughters' inherent strengths and then point out these strengths to them. It has also been important that my daughters see the connection between their strengths and a bunch of really good careers to pursue in the market, which play to those strengths.

This not only builds their confidence but gives them hope that they have a bright future in front of them. Yes, it is possible to make a good living and do work that you are proficient at and makes you happy. The alternative is to single mindedly pursue a lucrative and highly marketable career which requires you to convert many of your weaknesses into strengths. I think this is a surefire path to anxiety and despair.

At some point in our lives as parents, virtually all of us have told our children that they could become anything they want to be in their lives, as long as they put their minds to it. I've done it myself many times. We assume this is a way of telling our kids that we have faith and confidence in them. I think that the corollary to that statement is, "provided that whatever path you choose plays to your inherent strengths."

I've been preaching the futility of trying to turn other's weaknesses into strengths. Equally as damaging is pretending other's weaknesses don't exist or, worse yet, rewarding others for their weaknesses. In my youth, I spent most of my time playing sports in the schoolyard next to the elementary school I had attended. Back then there wasn't much in the way of organized sports with the exception of Little League baseball and Pee Wee football. Each day we would come home from school, drop off our books, put on sneakers and head over to the schoolyard. We would choose sides for, let's say, full court basketball. Eleven kids would show up, so someone would get left out because we usually played five against five. The conversation went something like this: "Louis, sorry pal but since we are playing five on five and eleven people showed up, you can't play." Louis might have responded,

"How come nobody picked me for their team?" Then someone would speak up and flat out say, "because you stink at basketball." To some of you this may seem to be cruel and insensitive. The truth of the matter was that Louis was a very weak athlete. Since we were all so competitive, it was all about winning for us. Our chances of winning dropped dramatically if Louis was on our team in any sport we played. Eventually, Louis stopped showing up at the schoolyard because he knew that no one wanted him on their team. I think he got the message that he was very weak in sports and that he was better off focusing on his strengths. He quickly figured out that athleticism was a personal weakness of his. As it turned out, Louis was a super smart student who became involved with a lot of clubs at school which played to his many strengths. I don't know what happened to Louis, but I wouldn't be a bit surprised if he moved out to San Jose, California and launched a high tech, start-up company and made a bunch of money. His schoolyard experiences quickly taught him that he was far better off focusing on his strengths as opposed to transforming his weaknesses into strengths. Good for him.

Today we live in a world where Louis would have been rewarded with a trophy for playing really bad basketball. He would have been led to believe that his weakness in basketball was actually one of his strengths. In other words, he would have been falsely rewarded for bad performance. Inevitably, however, his weakness would have been exposed. In my mind, it is far more cruel to lead someone to believe they are something that they are not, than it is to tell them in no uncertain terms that they stink in basketball. Am I alone in this thinking?

Let me shift gears for a moment. I'd like to tell you about my youngest daughter, Kate. She has spent most of her life paying very close attention to her two older sisters. This kid observed everything. There was no detail in her sisters' lives that went unnoticed. She not only observed their actions and behaviors but internalized these actions, which then became a standard for her in her everyday life. She was always the most gifted athlete in our household. I remember the first time she threw a ball and swung a bat. With no training whatsoever, she was a natural. She had those natural instincts and fast twitch muscles. Early on I was having delusions of grandeur. I was thinking to myself, "I don't need to save much for her college education. She's going Division 1 in women's softball on a full scholarship. It's in the bag." Not exactly. Her older sister was an avid dancer who danced six days per week for about 14 years. Unfortunately, the day came when Kate had to make the choice of giving up basketball or dance, both of which took place each Saturday at the same time. My natural athlete then made the decision to give up basketball, in no small part because her sister was a dancer. She ended up dancing six days per week for 14 years, just like her sister. This was a crushing blow to me. I now have a basement filled with a pile of unused baseball mitts, bats, basketballs, lacrosse sticks, frisbees, footballs, soccer balls and tennis rackets. Of course, there's no shortage of tap shoes, ballet shoes and dance outfits.

I'm digressing again. As I was saying, Kate observed and internalized every move her older sisters made. This placed a lot of pressure on her because her sisters were very gifted. They were excellent students, particularly in science and math. They were also very good test takers. Kate did not have these strengths. She was a good student but certainly not off the charts. She was ok in math and science. She was not a particularly good test taker. She knew this and felt a considerable amount of stress living up to her sister's natural strengths. To compound the problem, during her senior year in high school, several of her friends scored very high SAT scores and got accepted to schools such as NYU, Georgia Tech and Lehigh University. In her mind, she was thinking, "If I don't get great SAT scores, then I won't get accepted to a top University. If I don't get into a top University, then I will never get a high paying job. My prospects are even worse because I'm an average student in math and science. I will not make any money and will be forced to live with my parents until I'm fifty years old."

You know how this goes. You can start down a death spiral of completely irrational thoughts and soon sink into anxiety and hopelessness. So where am I going with this? As it turns out, this daughter of mine who had lived in the shadows of her siblings, has a list of strengths big enough to choke a horse. No, she will never win a Pulitzer Prize in Applied Mathematics. On the other hand, she has a great work ethic. She shows great empathy for others. She can engage in insightful, meaningful dialogue with just about anyone on the planet. She is a collaborative, team player. She is a natural born leader who can readily influence others in an assertive and appropriate manner. Yes, I'm bragging on her, but my point is that, in her mind, she doesn't necessarily see these strengths. What she sees are others' strengths which are her weaknesses. And these weaknesses threaten to deprive her of having a satisfying and productive career.

Here's where good parenting comes in. For my wife and me, the first step was making my daughter aware of her many strengths. Step two was pointing out that these strengths should be embraced as something to be very proud of. Step three was helping her understand that her natural strengths will lead to tremendous opportunities in the marketplace, even though she never achieved straight A's in math and science. We tell our daughter that she will be a great leader of people in whatever discipline she pursues. And there are a bunch of disciplines which play to her natural strengths such as digital marketing, sales, eCommerce, Human Resources, and Public Relations. I reminded her that her dad was a "B" student who was mediocre in math and science as well, but enjoyed a successful career, nonetheless. I also reminded her that I have had a whole bunch of "A" students in math and science who have reported to me over the course of twenty plus years.

In summary, here are a few things to keep in mind with your children:

- *Recognize their strengths*

- *Help them to become aware of these strengths*

- *Cherish and embrace these strengths*

- *Point out how these strengths can be aligned with career paths that will be very productive and satisfying*

- *Spend less time focused on their weaknesses and attempting to turn these weaknesses into strengths*
- *Love your kids for who they are and not who you had hoped they would be*

Capitalizing on Other's Strengths in the Workplace

As a leader in the workplace, there is a natural tendency to address others' weaknesses and attempt to either correct them or turn them into strengths. The problem is that those we are leading at work are no different than the children we are parenting at home. Converting their weaknesses into strengths is equally as arduous. In fact, capitalizing on their strengths becomes

even more important. The reason I say this is because, as leaders in the workplace, we are always trying to build a team. And some team members' strengths can help to compensate for other team members' weaknesses. That's part of what teamwork is all about, isn't it? Collectively, you can achieve great results by taking this approach, as opposed to attempting to change weaknesses into strengths. I have a great example of where I had failed to recognize this early on in my business career.

For nearly 20 years, I had a Vice President of Corporate Accounts who reported to me. He was one of the most unique and talented people I ever worked with in my business career. His strengths were off the charts -- as were his weaknesses. There was very little of what he did which was mediocre. He was either a superstar or really bad at stuff. For at least 10 of the 20 years that he reported to me, I attempted to coach him into making his weaknesses his strengths. For example, I tried to coach him into being a strategic planner and thinker. I also tried to coach him to train other salespeople to make them more effective at selling. In other words, I wanted him to multiply his selling ability through others. I failed miserably with both of these challenges. I frustrated the hell out of him by forcing him into doing things he was neither interested nor competent in doing. Worse yet, my failed efforts moved him further away from doing what God intended for him, which was going out into the market and selling better than any human being alive. I'm not exactly sure when it happened, but I woke up one morning and had an epiphany. I realized that I was trying to change him into something he is not. And in the process, I was discouraging him from focusing on his strengths and doing what he does best. At that point, I really backed off and stopped trying to turn his weaknesses into strengths. Instead, I embraced his incredible talent as a salesman, opened up the gate and let the big dog run. I honestly think he came out of his mother's womb with a natural talent to sell anything to anyone. Actually, he never thought of what he did as selling. Maybe that was the secret to his success. In his own words, he was providing his friends (everyone was his friend) with products that he felt were good for them. He was simply giving his friend what they need.

As I reflect on my career, I have run into many people who were merely "going through the motions" in the workplace. For them, work was a paycheck. Nothing more and nothing less. I cannot help but feel that they never fully recognized or capitalized on their natural strengths. That is really a shame. Life is too short.

Lesson Three

It's Not About You

Here's a lesson I've learned and unlearned hundreds of times. In reality, it may be more like thousands of times. In the previous chapter I referenced values, traits and beliefs, and the powerful influence they have on behaviors and actions. I also mentioned that I personally struggle with *selfishness,* which unfortunately, is not a trait conducive to good leadership or parenting. This trait of selfishness has led me to **behave selfishly** far too often in my lifetime. This is incredibly humiliating because I fully recognize the value of behaving unselfishly as a leader and a parent. When you are a selfish person, your natural tendency is to make everything about *you.* Conversely, when you are an unselfish person, your natural tendency is to put others first. For unselfish parents and leaders, it's about their children and those they are leading in the workplace. I have been working on becoming less selfish for as long as I can remember. For at least the past 30 years, when I blow out the candles on my birthday cake, I make the same wish, over and over again: to become a less selfish person. I've never admitted this to anyone before. Despite all of these birthday wishes, it has remained a struggle to consistently behave in an unselfish manner. Let me tell you, old habits die hard.

Here's an exercise which will give you a greater appreciation for how difficult it is to practice selflessness. First choose a person with whom you would like to be less selfish. It could be anyone. Then make a conscious effort to sit down with that person and commit to five minutes of unselfishness. This means trying to suspend your own thoughts, feelings, issues, and interests and completely focusing your energy and attention on the other person. Try to put yourself in their shoes. In other words, pretend that you are actually **them and not you.** If that were really the case, if you were them, how might you be feeling? What might you be thinking? What issues and challenges might you be facing? What hopes and dreams might be on your mind? During this five-minute period of time, you would probably not be talking very much. You'd probably be doing a lot of listening, observing and questioning. If you are one of the fortunate ones to possess the trait of unselfishness, then this exercise will not be very difficult to carry out. If you are like me, it is as painful as passing a kidney stone.

Unselfish Parenting

I'd like to start by discussing unselfishness, or selflessness, as it relates to parenting.

In my opinion, selflessness is a defining trait of a great parent.

A lot of what I have learned about being a selfless parent has been the result of being raised by very unselfish parents. For my parents, it was never about them. It was always about me and my sister. I never fully appreciated the extent of their selflessness until after they were gone. This is very disheartening. I would have liked to have thanked them for their selflessness and the extent to which they put my sister and I first in their lives. Interestingly enough, inasmuch as I've learned about selflessness through my parents, I have learned even more by observing my wife with our children. This woman is the epitome of selflessness and has been my greatest mentor on this subject. She has consistently demonstrated selfless behavior and actions as a parent each and every day of her life. It comes naturally to her. I first noticed this 28 years ago after she gave birth to our first child. She made a conscious choice to postpone her career as an eye doctor in order to stay at home with our daughter on a full-time basis. In her mind, the trade-off of pursuing her career and having the additional household income was far outweighed by the opportunity and privilege to be a full time Mom. I use the word "privilege" because we both recognize that many families do not have this option. I can recall multiple occasions when I would urge my wife to take a few hours to go shopping and treat herself to something she would like. Inevitably she would come back home with something for our daughters and nothing for herself. That's selflessness. My wife fully understands the concept of "it is not about you." The greatest example of her selflessness manifested itself by being an incredibly good listener with others, particularly with our children.

Stephen Covey is the author of a terrific book entitled, <u>7 Habits of Highly Effective People</u>. Habit 5 states: ***Seek First to Understand, Then to be Understood.*** I think this statement is brilliant and insightful. It implies a mindset focused on understanding others as a priority. This requires really good listening skills. If you possess an underlying trait of selflessness, it is a lot easier and natural to be a good listener. This is what my wife does each and every day of her life. Contrast this to someone who spends most of their time **trying to be understood.** Think about it. If you are running around all day trying to be understood, you're probably not doing much listening. You're probably doing most of the talking because you are trying to sell yourself and your ideas to others...**because it is all about you.**

Since I am a selfish guy, let's talk about **me** for a moment. Several years ago, I took my middle daughter on a field trip to visit the University of Michigan in Ann Arbor. I'm a huge fan of college football and basketball so naturally we visited the stadiums where the Michigan Wolverines play. I was completely awestruck by this experience. I was really pumped up and told my daughter, "Carly, this would be a great choice of schools for you!" I called my wife and said, "Honey, Michigan is perfect for Carly. Great football. Great basketball. Not far from the airport in Detroit. I could easily fly out to see a few games each year." Then my wife interrupted me and said, "Last I checked, Carly is not interested in football. She is not interested in basketball either. Tell me again why this is a good fit for our daughter?" Ugh. Once again, selfishness rears its ugly head.

All kidding aside, as a parent, I cannot emphasize enough how important it is to put children first. I think there are far too many parents that don't get this. It makes me wonder why they decided to have children in the first place. I can vividly remember an article I read in the *Wall Street Journal* in 1991. The topic was about saving for your kids' college education. I recall seeing a chart which projected the cost of a private college or university for the year 2010. After accounting for inflation, room, board and tuition was projected to be about $50,000 for a private college or university! I read this and nearly fell out of my chair. Remember, this was 1991 when the annual tuition for a private school was less than $15,000. I thought to myself, "there is no way I will be able to afford this, especially if I have two or three children!" My wife and I then made the commitment to save as much money as we possibly could from the day each of our children were born. We remained steadfast to this commitment for

25 years. This commitment also meant that we spent a lot less on ourselves during this time period. Again, **parenting is not about the parents. It's about the kids.**

It is shocking to me that so many parents spend a fortune on big houses, fancy cars and lavish vacations but save very little for their children's college education. To make matters worse, let's say your little Suzie gets accepted to Duke University. Unfortunately, Suzie doesn't qualify for financial aid and she did not earn a merit scholarship. Since you don't want to disappoint the little princess, you agree to send her to Duke anyway. Four years later she graduates with a degree in Eastern European Studies, along with $175,000 in student loans, which she may never be able to pay back in her lifetime. The good news is that you'll get to spend a lot of time with Suzie since she will have to live in your basement until she's 30 years old. This scenario is not far-fetched when you consider that there is nearly 1.5 trillion dollars of student debt in the US today. By the way, this is not a knock on Duke University. Duke is an elite institution. My point is this: if parenting is about the kids, and not about you, how is strapping your daughter with $175,000 in student debt for an undergraduate degree in *her* best interest? One last thing. Vanguard is one of the world's largest investment companies. They recently projected the total, four year cost for room, board, tuition and incidentals at a private college or university to be $500,000 in eighteen years from now. This is depressing. Who will be able to afford this?

Here's another example of, *it's not about you* as it relates to being a parent. Have you ever attended a sporting event and witnessed these maniacal parents carrying on in the bleachers? You know exactly who I'm referring to. Do you know why they are acting like jerks? That's right, you guessed it. They think it's all about them and not their children. They were probably mediocre athletes themselves and *are trying to live out their dreams through their children.* They also want to be able to tell their friends and neighbors how awesome their kids are in soccer because it makes them feel good about themselves. I played football in high school and college. As I reflect back, I realize that my dad never really commented on how good or bad I played. After a game, I'd ask him what he thought and he always responded the same way, "Steven, I'm glad you were not hurt out there." I didn't realize it at the time, but my Dad was looking out for my own welfare because *it was never about him.*

Unselfish Leadership

The personal trait of selflessness applies equally as well to leading others in the workplace as it does to parenting. The concept of unselfish leadership is really nothing new, although it has become popularized as of late. I think there is a strong similarity between unselfish leadership and Servant Leadership: a concept which is now in vogue. **_Servant leaders believe that they exist to serve their direct reports in the workplace._**

It's like turning the organizational chart upside down with direct reports on top and the leader on the bottom.

Traditional, authoritarian leaders, on the other hand, cling to the belief that their direct reports exist to serve them.

There's a popular school of thought which suggests that Servant Leadership is a more effective approach to leading others than authoritative leadership. Servant leadership is based upon the principle of influencing others through trust and respect. Authoritative leadership is based upon influencing others through fear and intimidation. Based upon three decades of leading others, and having been led by others, I'm convinced that Servant Leadership is the way to go. I have worked for both types of leaders in the past. My greatest mentor was a guy that practiced Servant Leadership on a daily basis. It was always less about him and lot more about his direct reports and creating an atmosphere for them to succeed. I can honestly tell you that I would have jumped off of a bridge for this guy. I trusted and respected him that much. He also placed his trust in *me* and I was highly motivated to never disappoint him. This was very powerful stuff. I have tried to emulate his style of leadership with my own direct reports for many years.

By the way, in my mind, Servant Leadership is not some wishy-washy approach aimed solely at trying to please others. It's really about getting results through others, but it's just as much about **how** *those results are achieved. Servant leaders develop and empower others around them to collectively contribute to results.*

Servant Leaders understand that it's not about them. It's about their direct reports. I have encountered many managers in my career that talked a great game about their self-proclaimed Servant Leadership style. In reality, however, they were anything but true Servant Leaders. I'll never forget one sales manager I worked with early on in my career. I remember him proudly proclaiming, "My people are my most important asset." First of all, what gave him the right to refer to his direct reports as "my people?" Who did this guy think he was, Moses? Also, if you would have seen this guy in action, it was always about him. It was never about the people around him. What was this crap about "my most important asset" anyway?

Before getting into further examples of Servant Leadership, I think it's important to start at 60,000 feet and ask yourself the question, "What is the role of

Leadership in my organization?"
Let's start with a quiz. Which of
these two statements most
accurately describes your
understanding of the role you play
within your organization as a
leader of others:

**A.   *Things you do that
     enable others to
        achieve results***

or

**B.   Things you do to
     achieve results**

If you answered "B", then you're
an idiot. I really didn't say that, did
I? That's just the sarcastic New
Yorker in me coming out. Seriously,
if you really think about it, "A" and

"B" are very different statements and imply very different leadership roles. To be perfectly honest, through most of my career as a leader, I viewed my role as **both** "A" and "B.". Towards the end of my career I shifted my mind set and behaviors more towards "A." I must admit that for me, it was a real adrenaline rush when I personally achieved results for the company. In addition, I always assumed that I was promoted to a leadership position to personally get things done. As I matured in my role as a leader, however, I began to realize that far more could be accomplished when my direct reports were collectively getting it done. In fact, the satisfaction I felt by seeing my direct reports develop and achieve results was greater than the adrenaline rush I would get by personally achieving results. (although it was close!)

Getting back to your responses from the quiz, you really are not an idiot if you answered "B." Answering "B," however, does say something about your own perception of what leadership is all about. In your heart, if you truly believe leadership is about **you** personally achieving results and getting these results turns your crank, you may be better suited to be a superstar, individual contributor rather than being a leader of others. Maybe this business about enabling and leading others to get things done and achieve results just is not in your wheelhouse. That's not necessarily a bad thing, by the way.

Oftentimes, really talented individual contributors get promoted into leadership positions. However, as an example, just because you are good at financial analysis, it doesn't mean that you will be a really good Chief Financial Officer.

First of all, leading others, regardless of the discipline you are in, requires a very distinct set of skills and competencies to be successful. It also requires a distinct set of underlying values, beliefs and traits which lend themselves to responding to "A" in the quiz. That is, you are more likely to see your role as one which develops and enables your direct reports to get results.

One of my daughters is a professional recruiter specializing in the IT field. She was recently being considered for a management position. When I spoke to her about the opportunity, she made some interesting comments to me. She said, "Dad, if I take the management position, I will have to spend a lot of time training and guiding others and it will take me away from what I really enjoy and do best, which is recruiting. Besides, the opportunity for commissions is greater as a recruiter than it is as a manager." It sounds like my daughter is more of a "B" than an "A." I was very proud of her response. At least she knows enough about herself to admit that management may not be the best fit for her at this point in her life. I think she showed a lot of insight and maturity. I can think of a lot of people who would have taken the management route without much thought because it sounds more prestigious. Let me tell you, the prestige wears off quickly, especially when you encounter "people problems" as a leader. You know what I'm talking about, don't you?

I have repeatedly referenced the role that values, beliefs and traits play on influencing behaviors and actions. In particular, it has been my experience that certain beliefs lend themselves nicely to being a selfless leader of others in the workplace:

Beliefs of a Selfless Leader

✓ *"I need them more than they need me"*

✓ *"I should be paid for what they accomplish and not for what I accomplish"*

✓ *"I succeed when they succeed"*

✓ *"I must do everything in my power to help them to be as successful as possible"*

All of these beliefs point to a mindset of selflessness. In other words, it's not about you. It's about your direct reports. It has been my experience that leaders who truly believe these things behave and act in ways that are consistently unselfish. I spent many years conducting training sessions on the topic of leadership with a focus on more of a selfless versus authoritarian leadership style. The purpose for the training was to build skills in selfless leadership, with the hope that training participants would then act and behave as selfless leaders. The dilemma I often faced was when training participants truly did not **value or believe** in the statements above. When that happened, the likelihood that they would change their behavior and apply the skills of a selfless leader was close to zero. At the time, I figured that I did a poor job of training but in reality, there is nothing I could have done about it.

For me personally, I always embraced the belief that I must do everything in my power to help my direct reports to be as successful as possible. I wasn't always great at it, but it was consistently a central focus for me as a leader. If you truly buy in to the belief that your role as a leader is to help others to succeed, then there is a high probability that you are *doing* the following on a daily basis:

- ✓ *Setting clear expectations and direction*
- ✓ *Eliminating obstacles*
- ✓ *Catching people doing things right*
- ✓ *Capitalizing on other's strengths*
- ✓ *Expressing trust and confidence*
- ✓ *Rewarding others*

✓ *Holding others accountable*

All of these things are ultimately aimed at developing others to reach as much of their potential as possible, while at the same time delivering results for your organization. I'll expand on many of these throughout the book.

Lesson Four

Do As I Do...Not As I Say

I'm sure you are familiar with the popular catch phrase, **"Do as I say and not as I do."** Parents are notorious for saying this to their children. I have a good story on this topic. When I was growing up, I remember every ashtray in our house being filled with ashes from Dad's Lucky Strike cigarettes. You may not be familiar with Lucky Strike. They were the most popular cigarettes sold in the US back in the 1930s and 1940s. Lucky Strikes or "Luckies" as they used to be called are unfiltered cigarettes. As if cigarettes are not bad enough for your health, the unfiltered kind are even worse. Apparently, this didn't matter much to my Dad who smoked at least a couple of packs of "Luckies" every day. He would say to me, "Steven, don't even think about taking up smoking. It's really bad for your health and could stunt your growth." Then I would say something like this: "but Dad, **you** smoke, so how bad could it be?" Then he would say, "Never mind that. I have my reasons for smoking. Just do as I say, not as I do." Although I never challenged my father on this topic, I remember thinking to myself, "isn't he being hypocritical?" In retrospect, I have come to believe that "do as I say and not as I do" may have been a very popular line but I don't think it ever really worked very well.

It has been my experience that *most people pay a lot more attention to what others actually do and not so much to what they say.*

I know that I personally do. I also think that most people can smell hypocrisy a mile away. As referenced earlier, hypocrisy is when people say one thing but do something totally different.

I think that *"do as I say and not as I do"* should be replaced with *"do as I do and not as I say."* I'd like to explore the relevance of *"do as I do and not as I say"* as it relates to parenting and leading others in the workplace. In case you were wondering, I never did take up smoking. My dad was diagnosed with early signs of Emphysema which could have killed him. Fortunately, he got the wake-up call and quit smoking cold turkey. It was a wake-up call for me as well as I never smoked a single cigarette in my life. This turned out to be a rare occasion when I did what my dad said and not what he did.

Do as I Do and Not as I Say... as a Parent

Years ago, there was a television commercial with a guy barking out instructions to his dog. From the dog's perspective, she really didn't understand a word of what her master was saying. All that she heard was, "blah, blah, blah, blah." I think this is relevant to parents barking instructions at their children as well. As parents we don't want to believe this, but a lot of what we say to our kids goes in one ear and out the other.

Children may not be paying close attention to a lot of things we say, but make no mistake about it, they are incredibly tuned in to what we do.

In fact, they are like little sponges, soaking up a massive amount of detail on every move we make. To make matters worse, they not only observe everything we do but they *internalize* our actions and behaviors. It's really scary when you think about it. With every move we make, we are giving them "programming" instructions which in turn, impact their internal beliefs, values and actions.

No pressure here, folks, but you might want to give a little more thought to what you actually do around your kids and not just what you say to them.

In parenting, as in life, it's a heck of a lot easier to **talk** a great game than it is to **have** a great game. I don't know what prompted this but the other day my youngest daughter turned to me and said, "I'll never forgive you for what you did to me at the beach." I raised an eyebrow and asked, "What are you talking about?" She told me, "You let go of my hand when the wave crashed in and I could have drowned."

Let me give you some background information on this incident. We used to vacation at Bethany Beach in Delaware for many summers. For whatever reason, the waves were always very aggressive at Bethany Beach. I taught my daughters that when big waves were approaching the shore, they had to make one of three choices. One choice was to swim over the top of the wave. Another choice was to dive under the wave. The third choice was to turn around, swim on top of the wave, and ride it on to the shore. There were no other choices. If you hesitated and did not choose any of these three options, really bad things happened. Anyway, fifteen years ago my daughter and I were staring down a wave and we didn't get our signals straight. I decided to swim over the wave, and she decided to dive under the wave. In the process, I let go of her hand and she was completely wiped out and came crashing onto the shore. Quite frankly I had long forgotten about this incident, but obviously I did something that stuck with my daughter for 15 years.

Again, as parents, we underestimate the extent to which our children are keeping

track of every single move we make.

If I would have realized this earlier in life, I can't help but think that I would have behaved differently around my children in many situations. On a side note, not only do kids observe every move we make with them, but they observe every move we make with **their siblings**. They are obsessed with this "fairness thing" as well. About seven years ago, our middle daughter, Carly, decided to call a meeting with my wife and me. We were seated at the kitchen table and she said, "I'd like to talk to you about the $100,000 you owe me." My wife and I were now staring at our daughter with a puzzled look on our faces. I then said to Carly, "We have no idea what you are talking about." I'll never forget her response for as long as I live. She replied, "I did the math and my college education will cost you $100,000 less than Emily's college education. I would like the $100,000 you owe me." Her math was correct because she had just decided on Penn State University and we were Pennsylvania residents. Her older sister, on the other hand, was attending Lafayette College which was a private school where the tuition was substantially higher. The conversation didn't end there. It got better. Carly then said, "Far be it for me to dictate to you *how* I should receive the money you owe me. It is totally up to you. You can pay me the difference in cash or you can buy me a car. Another option is warm weather vacations since it gets very cold at Penn State."

Folks, you can't make this stuff up. At this point my wife was looking at my daughter in utter disbelief. I was thinking to myself, "my daughter has lost her mind." Needless to say, we told our daughter that there was no way we owed her a dime on the difference between the cost of her education and her sister's education. She then responded: "As my parents, I thought you loved us all the same and had an obligation to treat us fairly." Can you believe this? I will admit, however, that I was thinking to myself, "this kid is good...really good. She is destined for a career in sales." I'll talk more about this in another chapter.

Getting back to "Do as I Do and Not As I Say"... As the father of three daughters, I worry myself to death about the guys they ultimately end up marrying. I must have preached to them a hundred times about finding a guy who truly loves them and treats them with respect. I could have said this a thousand times instead of a hundred times but, as I have been saying, kids pay a lot more attention to what we **do** as parents and far less to what we **say.** What if I preached to my daughters about marrying someone who will treat them with respect, yet they observe that I do not treat my wife with respect? Do you think they will buy the line, "do as I say and not as I do?" I don't think so. I've made a lot of mistakes as a parent but this is a subject of which I am most proud. My wife and I have always behaved respectfully towards one another. We believe that our kids have programmed this into their hearts, minds, and souls. My wife and I also work as a team with the understanding that we both have some things we do really well and some things we don't do so well. We then divide household chores based upon these strengths and weaknesses. For example, my wife is incredibly detail oriented and can balance our checkbook down to the last penny. Believe me, she will spend hours finding that last penny because, in her words, "it's a matter of principle."

Earlier in our marriage it was my responsibility to pay the bills and balance the checkbook. If I was within $100 of balancing our checkbook at the end of the month, I was perfectly content. I wasn't interested in using what little discretionary time I had available on chasing down a few bucks. Needless to say, I was soon relieved of this responsibility by the household's chief financial officer. This was fine with me. I'm the first to admit that balancing the checkbook was not a strength of mine. I'm more of a conceptual, big picture guy. Therefore, my wife manages the day to day budget, but I focus more on our long-term financial plan.

In reality, women control the money in most households anyway. Let's be honest. Earlier in my career I worked for

Mobil Chemical in Houston, Texas. One day I happened to pass by the Controller's office, and he was whispering on the phone to someone. He seemed very upset. I later asked him who he was talking with on the phone. He reluctantly told me that he was speaking to his wife and was asking her for an extension on his allowance for the balance of the week. I can't get this incident out of my head. I said to him, "Dude, are you kidding me? You are responsible for managing the money for a thirty billion dollar division of Mobil Oil and you have to ask permission from your wife for a ten buck extension on your allowance?" This was a great learning for me in life. Like I said, fellas, women control the money. Live with it and move on. By the way, in our household, there's none of this crap about, "women's work" or "men's work." Since I have recently retired, I do a lot more cooking and cleaning around the house. Why? Because it needs to get done and my wife is just plain tired of it. She had been carrying the load for a very long time and deserves a break.

I think our kids have picked up on this. I don't think male chauvinists stand any chance of earning our daughters' respect and affection. This reminds me of another funny story. I remember coming home from college one year to celebrate Thanksgiving with my family. I was at my aunt and uncle's house and we had just finished eating dinner. I got up from the table and started bringing the dishes into the kitchen. Within seconds I was confronted by my Uncle Sal who said, "What the hell are you doing? Are you trying to make us all look bad? What are they teaching you at this college of yours anyway? Now go sit down and watch TV with your cousins." That's too funny. Many years later I was in the kitchen and I got a text message from my wife who was watching TV upstairs in her "woman cave." In the text, she asked me to bring her a cup of tea and some cookies. Can you imagine if my Uncle Sal got this text message from my aunt? I would have paid good money just to see his reaction. In case you are wondering if I complied with my wife's request, the answer is simple: you're damn right I did. Do you think I'm stupid?

I'm digressing again. Another point about, "Do as I Do and Not As I Say": when my wife and I have our disagreements, we generally try to work them out behind the scenes. When we *do* have our disagreements in the presence of our children, we work them out in a respectful manner. Again, Do as I Do and not as I Say. I sincerely believe that this matters more to our kids than giving them the parent-child, "blah, blah, blah" message about the kind of relationship they should have with their future spouses. I have a friend that once gave me great advice on this subject. He suggested that when the time was right, that I take each of my daughters out on a "mock date" so that I can demonstrate how they should be treated. What a great idea. Open the car door for them before getting in the car yourself. Don't curse. Don't make the entire conversation about you. When ordering dinner, make sure her order is taken first. Don't talk with food in your mouth. Don't eat with your fingers unless it's pizza. This makes a lot of sense to me. It's another good example of "Do as I Do and not as I Say," right?

Do as I Say and Not As I Do as a Leader

"Do as I say and not as I do" has as much relevance to leading others as it does to parenting, if not more. I talked about the extent to which children watch every move we make as parents. As leaders, we are being watched every bit as much by those around us in the workplace. And the higher your leadership position in your organization, the more closely your behavior is being scrutinized. I know for certain that my actions in the workplace, many of which I considered to be completely innocuous, have been the topic of conversations at the dinner table by other employees at my company. If you are in a leadership role in the workplace, I promise you that the same thing is happening to you.

When you are promoted into a leadership position in your organization, you may not realize that you are now being perceived very differently by others. When you show up for work on the day after you've been promoted, you think that you are the same person that you were before you were promoted. Well, others around you don't view it that way. To them, you have become a different person who is now being held to a higher standard.

I remember a time soon after I had been promoted to the position of Vice President when I made a visit to the employees in our company's Pricing department. I said hello, thanked them for their hard work and asked them how things were going. At the time I was thinking to myself, "this is what I'm supposed to do as a Vice President." The next morning, I was made aware of a Pricing employee that I failed to greet when I was making my rounds. No big deal, right? After all, it was an honest mistake. Wrong. I quickly learned that the employee I failed to greet was devastated by my oversight. She thought that I disliked her and purposely ignored her when I was making my rounds. Worse yet, she thought that I didn't approve of her performance. She even asked her department manager if she was in jeopardy of losing her job. I'm sure she lost sleep over this and talked about the incident with her family and friends. When I found out about this, I felt terrible. I immediately met with her and told her that I didn't greet her for no other reason than that she was on the phone speaking with a customer and I didn't want to interrupt her. I told her that I was very appreciative of her hard work and support to the sales organization. She seemed appreciative and relieved after our conversation. This incident made me think of countless other occasions when my actions were probably scrutinized and interpreted by other employees at work. Since that time, I have always tried to be more consciously aware of my behavior in the workplace and the impact of these behaviors on others. A few months later I messed up again, but it was a lot worse. I walked up to one of our employees and said, "So how far along are you in your pregnancy?" She said to me, "I'm not pregnant." Wow. Awkward, to say the least. At that point, I was strongly considering **not** talking to female employees for at least a few years to ensure that I would no longer put my foot in my mouth.

Perhaps the greatest example of *"**Do as I Do, and Not as I Say**"* manifests itself when organizations undertake the daunting task of changing the company's culture. Billions of dollars are spent annually by organizations in an attempt to change the way they do business and achieve better results. Consultants are brought in to analyze the current business model and recommendations are made to make the organization more productive and efficient. Organizational structure changes are made. New business processes are put in place. Reward systems are revamped. Employees are re-trained on the new ways of doing business. Plaques, letterhead, logos and websites are changed to communicate the organization's new mission, vision and values. Most of you are well aware of what I'm talking about. It is often the case, however, that despite all of the time, money, and energy expended to execute all of these changes, in the end, it's still just business as usual. How can this possibly happen? As I've been saying, employees pay a lot more attention to what their leaders **do** and a lot less to what they **say.** If I'm the CEO and I talk a great game about the organization's new vision, mission and values but my behaviors, actions and decision making runs completely contrary to what I say, how do you think employees will react? Do you think if the CEO said to the rest of the organization, "Do as I say and not as I do," that others would buy into this? Not a chance.

I would like to point out that **"Do as I do and not as I say"** applies equally as well if you are a first level supervisor as it does if you are a *senior executive.* It always frustrated me at work when first level or middle level managers complained that senior managers and the CEO "talked the talk" but didn't "walk the walk." If you are the manager of the IT department, as an example, the employees that you are leading are looking as much to **you** as they are to senior executives. This means that they are carefully watching if **you** are "walking the walk" and not just "talking the talk." And if that is the case, then you have an obligation to behave and act in accordance with the company's mission, vision and values, even if the guy at the top is NOT.

At some point, you have to adopt the mindset of, "The buck stops here." In other words, stop bitching about others and start taking control of the things you can control. Start "walking the walk" and not just "talking the talk." That's what great leaders do.

I was blessed to have worked my last 21 years for a family owned, privately held company called Mannington Mills. The owner and Chairman of the Board at Mannington completely understood *"Do as I Do as not as I say."* Like many other companies, we had a mission statement and an explicitly communicated set of values. More importantly, all you had to do was to observe the behaviors and actions of this man to know exactly what was important to him. For him, it was maintaining a sensitive balance between profits and people and always doing the right thing. And believe me, our employees and even our customers were fully attuned to this. I would go so far as to say that our owner's commitment to behaving and acting in accordance to the company's mission and values gave us a competitive advantage in the marketplace.

I was so impressed by the company culture and the owner's commitment to maintaining this culture that I took it upon myself to protect and embody this culture through my own behaviors and actions. A funny thing happened as a result of this. I found myself surrounded by a management team that also behaved in a manner which protected the company's culture. For us, it was about doing the right thing and caring. It was also about what we called the "Five Fs": being Fast, Friendly, Focused, Fun and Flexible. Every one of my direct reports lived this. I was so committed to this that in 21 years as Vice President of Sales, I rarely fired a salesperson or sales manager for not hitting her numbers, but I fired a bunch of employees who didn't fit the company culture and values. My point is that I made a conscious effort to pay a lot of attention to my actions and behaviors, knowing that others around me were watching every move I made. For example, I **never** allowed myself to get drunk or out of control around **any** company employees and **never** around customers. Also, I always made myself accessible to my direct reports. When they emailed me or called me, I didn't care what time it was or what day it was, I tried my best to be responsive to them. Finally, I made an effort to act honestly and do the right thing with everyone surrounding me in the workplace, including customers. I know that my direct reports must have been paying attention to my actions because every one of them, in turn, acted the same way around others as well.

In summary, as a parent or leader of others in the workplace, there are countless opportunities, each and every day, to act in a manner that sets a good example for the people around you. And *acting* as a good leader and parent is a heck of a lot more meaningful and virtuous than *talking* like a good leader and parent.

Lesson Five

The Science of Constructive Dialogue

Most of us have watched "Jeopardy" on television. "Alex, I'll take Pioneers in Communication Technology for 600." "Ok, here's your clue: Antonio Meucci. Ray Tomlinson. Matti Makhonen." "And the question is, who invented the telephone, email and texting, respectively?" What? Huh? Who is this Meucci guy? Most people credit Alexander Graham Bell for inventing the telephone. In fact, many reliable sources credit Antonio Meucci for developing a voice communication apparatus which led to the very first telephone. Where am I going with this? I'm an Italian guy from Staten Island, New York. Antonio is an Italian guy who lived on Staten Island as well. When I tell people I'm from Staten Island, they invariably ask, "don't you have the largest garbage dump in the United States?" What people should be saying is, "didn't the inventor of the telephone live on Staten Island?" Way to go, Antonio.

Each of these talented men are credited for achieving magnificent milestones in how we communicate with one another. Most of us can't imagine everyday life without access to smart phones, laptops and tablets. These devices have forever changed the way in which we communicate. They have made us more efficient and productive. They have made the world smaller by keeping multiple cultures and geographies connected to each other 24/7. In a sense, they have also leveled the socio-economic playing field. Whether you are a billionaire or living below the poverty line, there is a good chance that you own the same type of iPhone as everyone else. All of these things are fantastic. Yet, in my opinion, despite all of the advantages that these magnificent technologies have brought us, there has been a very steep price to pay.

Unfortunately, these devices have now become a convenient substitute for constructive conversation between people. I'm talking about good old-fashioned, eye to eye, belly to belly, one-on-one dialogue with one another. And why is this even important as a parent or a leader of others? After all, we are all so busy. What's wrong with texting, emailing and skyping instead of communicating in person with others? What are we accomplishing in a face to face conversation that can't be accomplished in an email or text? A lot. A real lot. Studies on communications repeatedly indicate that **what people say is not what others hear.** This means that there is a breakdown in communications. When you are not face to face with someone else, you can't read their body language. You can't read their facial expressions. You can't read voice inflection. You can't look in their eyes. These are all important ways to determine if you and the person you are communicating with are truly on the same page. More importantly, these things reveal non-verbal signals which not only indicate if others **understand** what you are saying but whether or not they have **bought in** to what you're saying.

As a parent or leader, it is critically important to not only focus on the actual content of communications but all of this other stuff taking place. And this other stuff is nearly impossible to uncover through email and texting. Arguably, skyping is better than phoning which, in turn, is more constructive than emailing and texting.

What exactly does it mean when I say: "The Science of Constructive Dialogue?" Earlier I described parenting and leading as more of an Art than a Science. In the case of Constructive Dialogue, however, I view it as a specific task which conforms with scientific principles. Here's a useful definition of the word science:

"a systematically organized body of knowledge on particular subject"

I really do believe that constructive dialogue is both systematic and organized. I also believe that constructive dialogue leads to productive outcomes. In other words,

there is a systematic process which can be applied to everyday conversations with others which lead to productive results. This systematic process requires two essential building blocks, or skill sets, necessary to achieve constructive dialogue. One is listening. The other is questioning.

Listening and questioning are as essential to constructive dialogue as protein and fiber are for your diet. Unlike deeply embedded values, traits and beliefs, which are difficult to change, listening and questioning skills can be developed through repetition and practice.

Leaders and parents who possess these two fundamental skills are not only more likely to be good communicators, but just as likely to be good at parenting and leading as well.

Let's get into the details of these two fundamental skill sets:

Listening Skills

As a parent or leader of others, I cannot think of a more important skill set to possess than listening. The word "dialogue" infers that there is a healthy exchange of words between people. That means that both people in a conversation are doing some talking and some listening. If a parent or leader is doing most of the talking, there is a very good chance that constructive dialogue is not taking place. There's a reason why the good Lord gave us two ears and only one mouth. Maybe we were all meant to listen twice as much as we talk. As an example, when leaders interview candidates for an open job position, they should be talking less than 25% of the time. If they are doing all of the talking, how can they really know if the candidate being interviewed has the requisite skills to perform the job?

Another example applies to negotiating a deal as a salesperson. The best negotiators and salespeople let the other party in the conversation do most of the talking. This allows them to gather valuable information which can then be used to close the sale. I can't tell you the number of times I've been on sales calls where the salesperson would not stop talking. How can you really understand someone's business, the challenges they are facing and the opportunities in front of you, if you are talking 75% of the time? Trust me, I know what I'm talking about. For many years, I was the guy on the sales call that would never shut up. To make matters worse, I was the sales manager. So not only was I **not** uncovering opportunities for new business, I was undermining my own salespeople by talking over them during the sales call. What was I thinking? Ugh. In my defense, at least I learned from my mistakes.

There are several important components necessary for being a good listener:

Non-Verbal Listening

As listeners, whether we realize it or not, we are constantly sending signals to others about how much we respect and value them.

When you are engaged in a conversation with direct reports or your own kids, do you shut down your iPhone and give them your full attention? Are you squarely facing them with good posture? Are you establishing eye contact? When they say something you do not agree with, do you start rolling your eyes or folding your arms? Let's face it, we are all guilty of these things. I remember an incident with my wife as if it were yesterday. We were sitting in a hospital room moments before she went into labor. The television in the room was tuned in to Duke University basketball during the 1992 NCAA tournament. That was the year Duke featured players such as Bobby Hurley, Christian Laettner and Grant Hill. If you are a college basketball fan you know what I'm talking about. If you're like my wife, you couldn't care less. Anyway, my wife turned to me and asked me a question, just as Duke was about to score. Did I suspend my own self-interest and demonstrate good, non-verbal listening? Of course not. Instead I chose to look up at the TV and ignore my wife. Bad move. Very bad move. I wish I could turn back time and handle this differently. Poor non-verbal listening is a quiet killer, no different than high blood pressure. Most of the time, when you demonstrate poor non-verbal listening, others will not point it out to you. You could tell your children or direct reports, until you are blue in the face ,that you care about them, respect them and value their opinions. This means nothing. They will know how much their opinions are valued and respected based upon your demonstration of non-verbal listening.

Paraphrasing

As a listener, paraphrasing is simply summarizing, in your own words, what others are saying and feeding it back to them. It's another great way to let others know that you are truly listening. It's also a great way to keep the conversation focused. In fact, it's the only real proof others have that you have actually been listening. Now it's not necessary to paraphrase everything that others say. If someone says to you, "it looks like we may get some rain" and you say, "wait, let me make sure I understand you. You think we may be getting some rain. Is that right?" That would be a little creepy.

Reflecting Emotions

If paraphrasing is all about capturing a summary of what others are saying, reflecting emotions is all about capturing the feelings others are expressing. This is a very powerful technique for really connecting to others and showing empathy. For example, if you sense that someone seems really distraught over something as they are speaking to you, at some point you might say, "you seem really upset about this." Also, as either a parent or leader, when you are trying to influence someone to get something done, you can use the reflecting emotions technique to see if they really seem committed to accomplishing the task at hand. Their non-verbal language may indicate that they really do not seem excited or committed. You might want to call them out and say, "You don't seem too excited about this. What's going on?" Exploring this could be the difference between a task getting done effectively or not getting done at all. I have made the mistake on many occasions of not picking up on these non-verbal signals.

Taken together, non-verbal listening, paraphrasing and reflecting emotions are very powerful skills which contribute greatly to healthy, respectful and constructive dialogue with others.

To be clear, these really are *skills* which can be practiced and mastered over time, although it takes perseverance and hard work. Some personality types have a difficult time mastering listening skills. I am speaking from personal experience. Many years ago, I worked for Mobil Chemical and taught leadership and communication skills in many countries and languages. One of the workshops I taught was on Listening Skills. You would think I would be a pretty good listener, right? Wrong. Now I know the meaning of the expression, "those that can't do, teach." I can distinctly remember my wife noticing a Listening Skills binder sitting on my desk at home. She looked up at me and said, "Please don't tell me you actually teach this stuff to other people?" Yikes. That hurt. It is very frustrating because I clearly understand the importance of using good listening skills but apparently, I like to hear the sound of my own voice. This is something I continue to work on each and every day.

I cannot stress enough the importance of listening, particularly as a parent of three daughters. Sometimes my **lack of** listening has really caused problems. I remember many occasions when my daughters would be very upset over things which seemed so trivial to me at the time: "Dad, Jessica asked Caroline and Gina to go out for frozen yogurt, but she never asked me to go." I'm hearing this and thinking that it is no big deal. I would dismiss the problem by saying, "Carly, in the larger scheme of things, it's not a problem. Don't lose sleep over it." Well, in retrospect, my daughter was legitimately upset and although it seemed trivial to me, it really *was* a big deal to her. If it wasn't a big deal, she would have never brought it up. This was a big swing and a miss on my part.

Since I'm confessing my sins, I have another example of poor listening skills. Far too often my daughters, wife, or direct reports would tell me about a challenge they were facing. My immediate reaction was to start throwing out solutions to their problems. Sending solutions to someone is *not* a good example of listening. In fact, more often than not, others just want to vent and need a listening ear instead of a quick fix solution to make the problem disappear. Why do we do this anyway? I really don't know. Maybe we just want to be helpful. Maybe we want to feel relevant. Unfortunately, when we do this, we actually make matters worse.

Questioning Skills

The other fundamental building block necessary for constructive dialogue is questioning skills. There are **so many** benefits derived from asking really good questions. Good questions enable you to get valuable information from others. Good questions help you to understand others. Good questions allow you to assess others in terms of their competence and confidence. Good questions force others to think on their feet and take responsibility for their own actions. Good questions cause you to do less talking and more listening. All of this assumes, by the way, that you are asking good questions and then **shutting up** so that others can respond to your questions. This is easier said than done. We are all tempted to jump right in and seize control of the conversation. And eventually we say something stupid. I have done my fair share of this as well with my direct reports and children.

Some questions encourage others to open up and respond to you. These are often referred to as open ended questions. Open ended questions begin with words such as **what, how, when** and **why.** They encourage more than just "yes" or "no" responses from others. Closed ended questions, on the other hand, break down communications and get you "yes" or "no" responses from others. These are not good questions to encourage active, mutual dialogue. Close ended questions begin with words like **is, are, do** and **don't.** Good leaders and parents are very good at asking more open-ended questions rather than closed ended questions, which are next to useless when it comes to productive dialogue.

I have another funny story about open ended questions. When you raise teenage daughters, they go through a phase when they become very unwilling to share a lot of details about what is going on in their lives. At least that was our experience. I remember picking up my oldest daughter in front of a Catholic Boys High School where she was just leaving a dance party. She got in the car and I said to her, "Emily, tell me how the dance went?" Not a bad open-ended question, right? I'm thinking that we are about to have a lengthy and productive conversation. Instead, her response to me was: "Dad, please stop badgering me." How is that badgering? In my mind it wasn't even close to badgering. I wasn't even in favor of her attending the dance in the first place. The boy's high school only invited girls to the party. This strategy created what is known as a target rich environment. The boys far outnumbered the girls, creating an atmosphere where the girls competed with one another to gain the affection of the boys. Very clever. Devious, I might add, but clever, nonetheless. I never trusted those Catholic school boys. Then again, I never trusted **any** boys even remotely associated with my daughters.

In summary, taken together, listening and questioning skills are the fundamental building blocks for mutual, constructive dialogue with others. They are skills that can be developed and perfected through ongoing practice. As a parent and a leader, these skills are incredibly valuable in building relationships and healthy, truly interactive, two-way communications with direct reports and children. The use of these skills also builds trust, respect and good will, sometimes even with teenage daughters.

Lesson Six

Coach Your Heart Out

Coaching is another one of those critically important functions as a parent and leader of others in the workplace.

As important as this function is, many parents and leaders are not particularly good at it. Trust me, I am speaking from personal experience. Although I showed some signs of improvement later in life, I flubbed it pretty good in my younger days. As I have referenced repeatedly, actions and behaviors are heavily influenced by several factors, such as beliefs, traits and values, which are operating covertly all the time. As an example, if you possess the trait of selflessness as a parent and leader, then odds are that you dedicate a fair amount of time and energy coaching others to get better at what they do. Also, you are probably someone who gains as much satisfaction from developing others as you do from getting the job done **yourself.** Another factor influencing our ability to coach has to do with our understanding of the role we play, particularly as it relates to being a leader. For example, you may view your role as one of providing direction to your direct reports and either showing or telling them exactly what to do. If that is the case, you probably won't waste a lot of valuable time coaching others. On the other hand,

if your understanding of your role as a leader is to provide direction to your direct reports and to work with them to make them better, more confident and more self-sufficient in what they do, then chances are that you not only coach others, but are pretty good at it as well.

In addition to the many factors which influence our ability to coach others, the environment we are faced with also impacts our ability to coach. We live in a world where it is becoming increasingly difficult to be a really effective coach. That is because good coaching requires lots of time and patience, both of which are in short supply nowadays. Unfortunately, as parents and leaders, we are going a mile a minute and spending a lot of time putting out fires. The irony is that every minute we spend in "crisis mode" is a minute lost in coaching others to become more competent and self-sufficient. And the more competent and self-sufficient others become, the less time we are putting out fires. It is a frustrating, vicious cycle. I had been caught in this mess for a very long time and I'm the first to admit that breaking out of it is not at all easy.

What Is Coaching?

Before exploring the topic of coaching in more detail, let' start with a working definition:

Coaching is what you say or do to influence others to gain new knowledge, skills, confidence and self-sufficiency... resulting in the person being coached holding themselves accountable for the outcomes of coaching.

This is obviously a mouthful so let's analyze this in more detail:

"What you say or do"...

Coaching is oftentimes about what you say to others in the form of a conversation. For example, a discussion you have with a direct report who just made a mistake. Coaching can also be about what you do, or an *action* you take. For example, you might be demonstrating or role modeling to someone else how to do something. Sometimes coaching follows a methodical process where it's about what you say *and* do. For example, let's say you are coaching your daughter on how to change a flat tire. The first step in the process might be for *you* to demonstrate to her how to change a tire. In other words, your daughter is carefully observing what needs to be done. The next step is when you both participate in actually changing the tire. As a coach, this gives you the opportunity to assess how your daughter is performing the task. The final step is when you stop the "doing" and let your daughter do all of the doing. During this final step, although you are no longer "doing" anything, you are coaching her by having her "walk through" the steps she is taking to fix the tire. To me this three-step process makes a lot of sense.

"Influence others to gain new knowledge, skills, confidence and self-sufficiency"...

At the end of the day, coaching is really about doing whatever you possibly can to help others to get better and perform better. This could mean gaining new knowledge. It could also mean learning a new skill. *Perhaps most importantly, good coaches instill confidence in others as they are learning to improve their performance.* It's a funny thing about confidence. When someone's confidence grows, oftentimes their performance improves. The reverse is also true. When someone gains new knowledge and skills, their confidence grows. It's almost as though one feeds off of the other. That is why really good coaches not only influence others to improve their performance, but they pump others up and feed their confidence levels. Ultimately, as parents and leaders, we strive to make others more self-sufficient in everything that they do. After all, we are not going to be around forever, and we won't always be available to correct other's mistakes. At some point, we all want to push our direct reports and children out of the nest and watch them fly. Don't we?

"Holding themselves accountable for the outcomes of coaching"

The best coaches go beyond influencing others to gain new knowledge, skills, confidence and self-sufficiency. They also transfer the responsibility and accountability for owning new knowledge and skills to others as well.

This means that after you have coached your children or direct reports, they not only take pride in their higher level of performance, but they put it upon themselves to self-correct when their performance starts to slip, and they take full responsibility for the consequences of their actions.

It's almost as if your direct reports or children are performing not just because you want them to perform, but because they want to perform well for *themselves*. To me, this is where real commitment is achieved and, as a coach, you don't need to be hovering over them to ensure that things get done. It's the point where your children or direct reports become more independent, self-reliant and self-policing. And isn't that what we are really trying to reach as an end result? Or is it? I know a lot of parents and leaders that, deep inside, are not too crazy about this. After all, when others are coached up and take responsibility for themselves, what do they need us for anymore? Does this make us irrelevant? I have to say that I often missed this last step about transferring accountability to its rightful owner. It seems like the right thing to do, doesn't it? Yet, it is really difficult to do. This parenting and leading thing is not that easy. I'm one of those guys that views an awful lot of things as a process and coaching is no different. In other words, I believe that there is a step by step, systematic approach for coaching others which inevitably leads to really good outcomes.

The 5 Step Coaching Process

Many times, coaching is nothing more than a conversation with others. Here are five useful steps to take for having an effective coaching conversation. Please note that there are neither 4 steps in the process nor 6 steps in the process. There are exactly 5 steps in the coaching process. If you don't follow these 5 steps, in sequential order, then you have failed miserably as a coach. (Not really. I'm joking with you.)

- *State Purpose for Coaching*
- *Solicit Input*
- *Listen*
- *Provide Feedback*
- *Summarize and Discuss Next Steps*

Let's review each of these 5 steps in more detail:

State Purpose for Coaching

I know this probably seems obvious, but it really isn't. How often have you been in a meeting or discussion with someone else and you are asking yourself: "What am I doing here and what is the purpose for this?" This happens all the time. It never hurts to be up front and state the purpose for the discussion which is about to take place. For example, you are a financial manager and you are not pleased with the analysis done by one of the accountants for the quarterly close. You might start the conversation by saying, "The purpose for this meeting is to review the analysis done in preparation for the quarterly close." Plain and simple. It sets the tone and direction for the meeting. It also leaves no doubt as to why you are having the meeting in the first place.

Now I'd like to contradict what I've just said. As parents, oftentimes coaching children (especially teenage daughters) can be tricky. I'm convinced that my daughters are equipped with radar which alerts them when I'm preparing to coach them. Before I even open my mouth, they become defensive and they don't even know what the topic of discussion is all about. I know I'm not alone in facing this experience. Once kids get in this defensive mode, it is very difficult to coach them. Things start getting irrational, emotional and stupid. Not an atmosphere conducive to productive coaching. If your daughter is on to you and knows that you are about to "coach her up" for let's say, her excessive partying at college, she may not be very coachable. In my experience, there is an art to finding just the right time and place to dial in to a channel where you get good reception with your children. I remember when one of my girls turned 21 and we sat at a bar in a local restaurant. Somehow our relationship changed from parent and child to a couple of friends knocking down a few drinks together. The atmosphere was totally different. Suddenly there was a higher level of trust, openness and certainly much less defensiveness. I remember learning so much about my daughter as a person, and not just as my daughter. Maybe she began to see me as a person as well, and not just the old man. There was a window of opportunity to coach her and she didn't even know she was being coached. It was a beautiful thing. Of course, when we left the bar, we reverted back to our traditional roles again. It was still a win in my eyes. I connected with my daughter and knocked down a few beers in the process.

Solicit Input

This is big. Really big. This is coming from someone who has swung and missed on far too many occasions.

One of the worst things you could do as a parent and a leader is to initiate a coaching discussion by completely unwinding on others.

In other words, you sit them down and rip them apart by telling them all of the things they screwed up, and all of the ways they have let you down. By the way, there is a time and a place in the coaching process to do this, but you never come out of the gates this hard, at least not initially. I can give you several reasons why this is a bad idea. First, you'll probably get the other person so wound up that they will not be in a very receptive mode to listen and be open-minded about learning from their mistakes. Second, soliciting input from others gives you the opportunity to assess their understanding of the issues and their level of commitment to resolving those issues as well. Getting back to the example of the quarterly financial close, the manager could start by asking the accountant, "In your opinion, how do you think the analysis went in preparation for the quarterly close meeting?" The door is now open for the accountant to share his response to the question. If the manager is listening, she will pick up very useful information about the accountant's skill, knowledge level *and* level of commitment to doing really good analysis in preparation for the financial close meeting. Another good reason for soliciting input is to help the person you are coaching to save face. Using the same example as above, if the accountant has the opportunity to point out mistakes he has made, it is always better than having your mistakes pointed out by your manager.

I'm going to contradict myself again by saying that there are circumstances under which the approach I've outlined above is actually the *last* thing you want to do. Suppose that you are a Captain in the Fire Department. You enter a burning building with a rookie fireman who is about to make a bonehead move which could kill both of you. That *is not* a good time to coach the rookie and patiently solicit input from him. In fact, that approach could get you both killed along with everyone else in the building. When you return to the firehouse, however, it would be much more appropriate to employ these coaching steps.

Listen

I referred to listening as a critically important communication skill in the previous chapter. It's worth reviewing again because good coaches are typically very good listeners. When you are coaching one of your direct reports or children, and you are soliciting their input and ideas, listening becomes extremely important. It means zipping up and not interrupting. It means that you are not jumping in to evaluate what others are saying. It means you are not offering advice or solutions. Instead, you are trying to be patient enough and disciplined enough to allow others to speak their mind, whether you agree or disagree with what they are saying. This is very difficult to do in practice. It goes back to the expression coined by Steven Covey, *"Seek First to Understand than to be Understood."* It's also about suspending your own thoughts and feelings because at this stage in the coaching process, *it's not about you, it's about them.*

Provide Feedback

After you have patiently taken the time to hear other's points of view, even though it feels like your heart is about to explode, it is then time to provide feedback to others. And there is a very big difference between providing constructive feedback and destructive feedback to others.

Constructive feedback should always be focused on a specific task, problem or situation and should never be focused on attacking someone personally.

For example, suppose your daughter comes home from college for the summer and treats your household like it's a Courtyard Marriott. She throws her towels on the bathroom floor. She doesn't make up her bed. She doesn't help set the table for dinner. Mind you, this is purely hypothetical and would never really happen. (Oh, the pain). You've had just about enough of this nonsense and decide to give your daughter some feedback. You can go in one of two directions on this. One direction is to get really personal and attack her character: "Carly, you have to be the laziest, most inconsiderate human being on the planet." I don't know about you, but I've thought about saying this to my kids on more than one occasion. Let me correct that. I **have** said this to my daughters. The other direction you could take is to address the specific behaviors which are problematic: "Carly, every night when we are ready to have dinner, you never help set the table. Your mom and I are getting very frustrated with this. We expect that you will take the initiative, without having to be asked, to set the table before we have dinner." In my opinion, direction number one is not helping anyone, although it might make you feel better. It's attacking the other person's character which could be very devastating. Chances are pretty good that if you gave your daughter this type of feedback, you would not only alienate her, but there is very little chance that anything will change in her behavior. In fact, her behavior could get **worse**.

Another key to providing others with feedback is to be very specific with your wording. Back in high school, I used to work at my uncle's delicatessen. He was never shy about giving me feedback. His favorite line was, "Steven, you have a bad attitude. You need to straighten up." What the heck was I supposed to do with this? Until this day, I have no idea what he was talking about. He was not specific with the behavior which he considered problematic. Can you imagine visiting your primary care physician who examines you, shakes her head and says, "If I were you, I'd think seriously about getting yourself healthy." This is ridiculous, isn't it? If your doctor said this to you, what would you do differently when you left her office?

One day I was golfing with some guy who was complaining about his boss. He told me that he was the worst manager he had ever worked for in forty years. I asked him why his boss was so bad. He said, "My boss tells me that my business strategy is flawed and that it will never work. Then I asked him what I could do to adjust my strategy to be more successful. He then says he has no idea. All he knows is that my plan is really bad." Boy, was this guy pissed off. After he finished telling me the story, he shanked his drive about a mile into the woods. Be honest, do you think you have ever given your children or direct reports feedback which was over the top vague and attacked their character? It happens all of the time. Heck, we've all been on the receiving end of this crap and did it turn our performance around? More than likely it made a bad situation worse.

Perhaps the most important attribute of providing constructive criticism is to do it in the spirit of care and love and genuinely wanting to help someone to get better. The opposite of this is providing feedback to someone to tear them down, humiliate them and cause them to lose confidence in themselves. Good parents and leaders are never coaching others and providing feedback with this intent...***ever!***

I'm a big fan of college basketball. I was watching a Michigan State game during a recent NCAA Tournament and their coach, Tom Izzo, was really jacked up on the sidelines. He was screaming at one of his players to the point where other players and coaches had to pull him away from the scene of the incident. Clearly, he was not following the coaching process outlined above. The following day, in the news, there was a lot of debate and controversy as to whether or not Coach Izzo was verbally abusive to his players. Interestingly enough, a number of sports analysts and former players came to his defense and explained that he truly loves his players and coaches them with the sole intent of helping them to get better at the game of basketball. When he gives them feedback, it is not aimed at attacking their character as human beings. It is targeted at specific behaviors and actions taken by the players in order for them to perform better. Would you consider Tom Izzo's action to be representative of good coaching? Interesting.

Summarize and Discuss Next Steps

This is the final step in the coaching process. It is also an opportunity to transfer accountability to the person you are coaching. Towards the conclusion of a coaching conversation, it is a good practice to turn to your direct report or child and have them summarize the conversation and articulate the immediate next steps which have to take place. This gives you the opportunity to gauge their understanding and commitment to the coaching topic. More importantly, they are given the opportunity to tell you how they will hold themselves accountable for following through on the coaching topic as well. By the way, this last step could go either way. Your child or direct report may send you verbal and non-verbal signals which indicate that they are not the least bit motivated to change their behavior or hold themselves accountable for their actions. Although this is painful to hear, this is good to know because it tells you that your work as a coach is far from being done. Like I have been saying, this business of leading and parenting others is really tough work.

One last thought on this topic. Timing really matters when it comes to coaching. It does no one any good to receive feedback and get coached six months after the opportunity to provide coaching has taken place. Recently my wife provided me with "constructive criticism" about a comment I made in front of her parents nearly 30 years ago. Why am I finding out about this now? If I would have known about this much sooner, I could have done something about it 30 years ago. By the way, how could my wife even remember a comment made 30 years ago? I can't even remember what I ate for breakfast three days ago. A classic example of the importance of timing when coaching others and providing feedback.

Another example of the importance of timing has to do with the traditional practice of conducting annual performance appraisals. Many organizations have a formal process of evaluating employee's performance on an annual basis. Sometimes mid-year reviews take place in addition to a final end of year evaluation. In reality, coaching and providing others with feedback on their performance should be happening on an ongoing basis as the need presents itself. By the time the annual appraisal discussion takes place, there should be absolutely no surprises. It is way too late to hear about your poor performance in February at the appraisal meeting which takes place 10 months later in the year. In reality, however, this is not how it works in the real world with many companies. I remember a former manager of mine preparing me for our annual appraisal meeting. He started the conversation by saying, "Steve, think of feedback as a gift...and today is Christmas." Nice.

In summary, coaching is a vital function for any good parent or leader. Coaching is a process of influencing others to gain new knowledge, skills and confidence. It's also about helping others to become more self-sufficient and hold themselves accountable for the outcomes of coaching. When coaching others, it's always a good practice to get them engaged in the coaching conversation and then shut up and listen. This helps you to assess their level of competence, confidence and the extent to which they are committed to holding themselves accountable. Baby boomers are always complaining that the younger generations, most notably the Millennials, are a "different breed." They are disrespectful. They have no work ethic. They seek immediate gratification. They want to be promoted to Vice President without being willing to put in the time and energy to earn the position. In my opinion, this is not entirely true, at least in my experience. Yes, we live in a very different world today than we did in 1980 and technology has changed things dramatically. That being said, there's a bunch of stuff that has not changed at all. For example, the majority of employees in the workplace want to know what is expected of them. They want to be good performers and they seek feedback and coaching to help them to get better. They want these things whether they are Baby Boomers, Millennials or Generation Zs. Similarly, children will always need solid parents who provide them with direction and support to help guide them into adulthood. Employees in the workplace always need ongoing direction and support from their leaders in order to get better at what they do. As leaders and parents, let's not let them down.

One other thing, through the years, I have discovered a very tight correlation between adult learning theory and really good coaching. Consider this: **when adults learn new things, they retain:**

10% of what is read

20% of what is heard

30% of what is seen

50% of what is seen and heard

70% of what is discussed with others

80% of what is experienced

95% of what is being taught to others

Coaching involves the transfer of knowledge, skills and accountability to others. If your coaching style is all about lecturing your direct reports and children, and nothing more, according to adult learning theory, they will retain only 20% of the skills and knowledge you are attempting to transfer to them. On the other hand, suppose your coaching style is all about allowing others to experience failure, followed by a two-way coaching discussion so they can talk through their own experiences. If that is the case, then there is a greater likelihood that their retention rate on the new skills and knowledge they are learning will *quadruple.* That is pretty amazing!

Lesson 7

Providing Big Picture Direction

Some people in life are blessed with the trait or characteristic of seeing the big picture. This is truly a gift and one that is not easily learned. In my opinion, it is another one of those traits that people are born with. This is not to say that Big Picture Thinking cannot be learned. It can, but it is not that easy. If you are fortunate enough to possess this gift, it will serve you extremely well as both a parent and leader. That being said, oftentimes our strengths can also be our weaknesses. Many big picture people lack attention to detail, which can be a problem in and of itself. I know a handful of people that are both big picture thinkers *and* detail oriented. This is a deadly combination of strengths, especially if you understand **when** it's appropriate to fly at 60,000 feet and when it's time to take the chopper down to six inches above the ground. For some professions such as accounting and cardiovascular surgery, detail orientation is a far more valuable trait to possess than big picture thinking. When it comes to leading others and parenting, one can make the argument that detail orientation *and* big picture thinking are equally important traits to possess. In my opinion, however, big picture thinking is as important to being a good parent and leader as detail orientation is to being a good accountant or cardiovascular surgeon.

Providing Big Picture Direction as a Leader

Earlier in my career I was fortunate enough to have worked for one of the most talented CEO's on the planet. He was one of those guys that I just described: incredibly intuitive about when to focus on the big picture and when to dive into excruciating detail, in order to keep the business on track. I remember multiple occasions when we would all be sitting around the table in a conference room. We would go around in circles trying to solve a business problem. Our CEO would sit back, listen and analyze what was being said. It was almost as if he could remove himself from his surroundings...like he was floating above the room. I know this sounds weird but that's what it felt like. Then at some point he would speak. It was like the EF Hutton commercial: "When EF Hutton talks, people listen". Do you remember that commercial? Our CEO was like EF Hutton. He would speak and then something amazing would happen. He would somehow sift through a ton of random information being thrown around and inevitably get to the root cause of the problem. He was always fact-based and kept subjective opinions and emotions out of the discussion. More importantly, he provided high level clarity and direction in the midst of a crap storm filled with random bits of seemingly unrelated information. The result of all of this was crystal clear focus on only a select few actions that, when taken, would not only solve a bunch of micro problems, but would give us the best chance of solving the really big problems.

The approach taken by my CEO was very energizing. It also kept our time and energy laser focused on efficiently working through the real problem which, in turn, inevitably led to optimal results for the organization. It is a great example of big picture thinking and providing both direction and leadership to others. Employees long for this type of direction. In the absence of this type of leadership, most of us mortals spend an inordinate amount of time and energy getting caught up and often stalled in minutia. In this minutia, we are trying to win a ton of small battles but we never getting closer to winning the overall war. As leaders, there are times when we have to pull ourselves and others out of the weeds and demonstrate big picture thinking. If we do not fulfill this function, then who will?

This reminds me of another story. Are you familiar with a company called Golftec? They provide a service to golfers by analyzing golf swings and subsequently providing lessons to correct golf swings. They also recommend and sell golf clubs which are best suited to complement golfers' swings. They are very good at what they do. Anyway, some friends of mine gave me a gift certificate to Golftec. I remember my wife saying, "What a thoughtful gift your friends have given you." In reality, there was nothing thoughtful about it at all. My friends couldn't bear the pain of watching one more day of my miserable backswing. On my first visit to Golftec, the instructor strapped me into a waist and shoulder harness which was electronically attached to a monitor. Sort of like an EKG machine, which is used to monitor heart activity. In this case, the monitor is designed to evaluate your golf swing. Anyway, I'm all hooked up and I proceed to take some practice swings by hitting golf balls into a large canvass. Then I'm presented with about 700 numbers, most of them in red, posted on a flat screen projector. I said to the instructor, "What are all of these numbers?" He explained, "We have been able to evaluate every aspect of your golf swing: how you are turning, twisting and bending your shoulders, back, hips, knees, neck and head." Then I said,

"There's a sea of red numbers on the screen. I take it that red is bad." He said, "Yes, red is bad. Really bad." Great. In other words, my golf swing is an absolute train wreck! At that point I'm thinking to myself that I'd be better off canning golf and taking up bowling.

It gets worse. Apparently, one of my countless flaws is that I separate my elbows during my backswing. The instructor then proceeds to superimpose a professional golfer, Hunter Mahon, next to me on a split screen. Hunter is the best in the business at keeping his elbows together in his backswing. I then got to watch his backswing and mine at the same time, in slow motion. Oh my God. It was like watching a weightlifting competition between Arnold Schwarzenegger and

Woody Allen. In that moment I discovered Golftec's competitive advantage: humiliate your customers and guilt them into paying a thousand bucks on lessons so you don't look like a moron on the golf course. By the way, I paid the thousand dollars for lessons and I'm a better golfer, thanks to Golftec.

I'm digressing yet again. Here is where I'm going with this. I remember telling the Golftec instructor that I was overwhelmed by the number of defects in my golf swing and that there was no possible way I could correct these defects all at the same time. Here's where the epiphany took place. My instructor said, "We are not going to try to correct all of your flaws. There are only two things we will focus on. One is related to your stance and one is related to your backswing. If you master these two things, not only will this correct fifty other defects, but it will lead to better results in general. In fact, it will reduce your scores by five to seven strokes, on average." When he said this, I had flashbacks of my CEO. He used to do the same thing! That is, **analyze the situation or problem, and focus others on one or two things that, if executed on, would not only solve a bunch of micro problems, but would solve the really big problems and yield optimal results for everyone.**

By the way, I'm amazed at the number of people who invest a ton of money in technology, instead of investing in lessons to improve their golf game. Recently I was golfing with a guy who had equipment which must have been designed by NASA. His golf swing, however, made mine look like Tiger Woods'. I felt like telling him, "Listen, pal, if we put Albert Einstein, Isaac Newton and Galileo in a room together, they couldn't build you a club to compensate for that crap swing of yours." The New Yorker in me is coming out again.

To summarize, it is a blessing and a gift to possess the trait of big picture thinking. Far too many leaders are lacking in this trait and those they are attempting to lead end up suffering the most. As I have said earlier in this book, the overwhelming majority of employees want to do a good job. They want to do the right thing. At the same time, they become frustrated and despondent when they feel like they are spinning their wheels and working like a dog with nothing to show for it. Good leaders have the insight to see the bigger picture, get out of the weeds and direct other's efforts onto the really important stuff which leads to efficient and productive results for everyone.

Big Picture Direction as a Parent...

Kids today get bombarded with advice and guidance from a multitude of sources: parents, grandparents, coaches, teachers, ministers, older siblings...the list goes on and on. Oftentimes, the advice and direction provided from these sources is contradictory. It can be overwhelming for our children. It can also be overwhelming for parents who are trying to keep their kids on the straight and narrow path.

As a parent, if you are not a big picture thinker, it is easy to micro-manage every aspect of your children's lives. Although the intent is usually noble, the impact of this type of parenting can be damaging. Just like employees in the workforce, the children we are parenting long for big picture direction. In other words, what's the really important stuff that they need to get right to be a solid citizen in society? For my wife and me there were just a handful of big picture guiding principles which we tried to instill in our children and not sweat the small stuff (in reality, we never stopped sweating the small stuff either, especially my wife):

- *Use Good Judgment when Making Decisions*
- *Know Right from Wrong*
- *Respect Yourself and Others*
- *Work Hard*
- *Don't Take Drugs*

In my opinion, if kids internalize these five principles, everything else will take care of itself. Let's use an example. Let's say you micro-manage many aspects of your son's life. When he wanted to dye his hair blue, you successfully dissuaded him. When he got his driver's license and wanted to take a road trip to California during the summer with his buddies, you successfully talked him out of it. When his grades temporarily dropped from "A"s to "B"s, you coached him up and got him back on track. Let's also say that your son has a tendency to use really poor judgement. Unless you are on his case, his work ethic is sorely lacking as well. He also does not show others common courtesy and respect. If you were rated on your parenting skills, what score would you give yourself in the above scenario?

Now let's use another example. Let's say your daughter is a really good kid but she's carefree and a bit mischievous at times. You also believe her jeans are way too tight, but you stay off of her case. Some of her grades are not as good as you would like to see but she does put in the time studying so you don't push her too hard to maintain straight "A"s. Her room is a complete disaster, but you don't threaten to throw her out of the house unless she cleans it up. All of this being said, she is a poster child for the five principles above. What score would you give yourself, as a parent raising your daughter? I think this is a no brainer. Pat yourself on the back for excellent parenting. To me, this is putting some wide guard rails in place and leaving some wiggle room for them to just be themselves and not do everything in their lives one hundred percent "by the book." I think back on many occasions when I got caught up in the weeds and tried to micro-manage my kids on stuff. In the larger scheme of things, this stuff was small potatoes in comparison to getting the "big five" above right. I remember getting upset with my kids because they did a crappy job of properly spacing the ornaments on our Christmas tree. Really? That was really dumb on my part. By the way, big picture direction has a much better chance of working if you, as a parent, live and breathe these five principles in your own life. As I have been saying, kids pick up on what we do a heck of a lot more than what we say.

Lesson 8

Influencing with Rewards and Recognition

Can I get a show of hands from those of you with children? Keep your hand up if your child's bedroom would be condemned by the local Board of Health? I sense a I lot of hands in the air. Honestly, where did we go wrong? Maybe you are one of the lucky ones who hasn't lived with this curse. God bless you.

Our middle daughter's bedroom has been a pig sty for as long as I can remember. We were hoping things would miraculously change when she returned home after being away at college. Nothing changed. Actually, her room actually got worse, which I didn't think was humanly possible. She would actually lay on the bedroom floor, form a pillow out of random pieces of clothing lying around and place them behind her head while working on her laptop. It was so bad that my wife would simply shut her door and pretend that her room didn't even exist. For years we had the same conversation with our daughter about her room: "Carly, how difficult can it be to either hang your clothes in the closet or fold them and return them to your dresser? If your clothes are dirty, then put them in the hamper. Why do you just throw all of your clothes on the floor?" This conversation went nowhere, and her behavior did not change. Then we made the discussion more personal: "How can you live with yourself? Don't you take at least *some* pride in your own personal hygiene?" This didn't work. Then we tried to threaten her: "If you don't keep your room clean, we are cutting off your tuition at Penn State." This didn't work either. Our daughter was astute enough to know that we would have never followed through on this threat. She was right. We kept having the same conversations with our daughter, over and over again, yet the results never changed. This is the classic definition of insanity.

I started thinking about what it would take to finally alter my daughter's behavior and then it hit me. This kid was highly motivated by cold, hard cash. We learned this about her from a very early age. When she was ten years old, she played in a local basketball league. Every Saturday I watched her from the stands hoping that, one day, she would actually score a basket. It was very frustrating because she would consistently run down the court and pick a spot under the basket, but she wouldn't move. She would never try to break free and get open. Therefore, no one ever passed her the ball so she could even attempt to score a basket. Even when the ball was passed to her, she refused to take a shot and would pass it back to another player. For most of the season, I would yell from the stands, "Carly, move around! Carly, get open. Carly, shoot the ball!" Nothing. No behavior change, whatsoever. I couldn't stand it any longer. I finally decided to bribe her with money and told her, "Carly, I'll pay you three bucks for every basket you make during next Saturday's game." Lo and behold, just minutes into the game, my little Michael Jordan makes a basket. She sees me in the stands and holds up three fingers to remind me that I owe her three bucks. I know that my bribes were a shameless example of good parenting, but I didn't care. I was pretty pumped up. Guess what happened a few minutes later? You are correct! She scored her second basket. Guess what happened a few minutes after that? You are correct again: another basket and nothing but net. You get the point.

Here's an example of a type of reward which influenced and shaped my daughter's behavior.

Let's fast forward nine years later to my daughter's' train wreck of a bedroom. Hard cash motivated her behavior before and maybe it would motivate her to keep her room clean as well. So instead of engaging my daughter in yet another useless conversation about cleaning her room, I decided to say nothing to her. Instead, I taped a four-month calendar for May, June, July and August on her bedroom door. The very next morning I checked her room and, as expected, it looked like ground zero for Hurricane Irene. I then proceeded to post a very large "2," in red, in the box labeled May 10 on the calendar. The following morning, I repeated the drill and my daughter's room failed inspection, so I posted another big "2," in red, on the calendar for May 11. On the evening of May 11, my daughter said to me, "Why is there a calendar on my door and what's with the red "2s"?" I replied, "That's a very good question, Carly! It means that you owe me two bucks for May 11 and two bucks for May 12." She then asked, "What are you talking about?" I told her, "For every day that your room is a mess, you owe me two dollars." Here's the punch line. I then added, "On the other hand, for every day that your room is clean, I **owe you** two dollars." So, what do you think happened? My daughter's room passed inspection on every single day for the rest of the summer. No more emotional discussions about keeping the room clean. For my daughter, money talks and until this day remains a powerful motivator in her everyday life. It is no wonder that today she is a salesperson working off of straight commissions.

Before going further, I'd like to define the terms **Reward** and **Recognition** and make a distinction between the two:

Reward

"a thing given in recognition of one's service, effort or achievement"

Recognition

"acknowledgement of achievement, service, merit, etc."

Let's start by exploring the term *Reward* in more detail. In the definition above, a reward is described as a "thing given in recognition of one's service, effort or achievement." This "thing" typically has some monetary value. It can be cash, gift certificates or some other material item which has cash value.

There has been a raging debate for centuries as to whether or not cash, or cash equivalent, rewards can actually influence people's behavior. There is no simple answer to this question. I do know that human beings are very complex and that no two people are exactly alike in terms of being motivated by monetary rewards. For example, our youngest daughter's room was as unkempt as our middle daughter's room. Since monetary rewards worked with one daughter, why wouldn't they work with another daughter? I implemented the very same reward program for my youngest rug rat with less than stellar results. She was not the least bit motivated to change her behavior for a few bucks. In addition, she was more than happy to have her allowance docked as opposed to going through the trouble of keeping her room neat and clean. I soon learned a valuable lesson that not everyone responds the same way to monetary rewards. This includes my own children. Why is it that our own children are so different from each other? We really didn't raise them that differently, did we? This will always remain a mystery of life for me.

I have another funny story on this topic. My wife and I currently live in Pennsylvania. Our oldest daughter lives in Ohio. Our middle daughter lives in California. Neither of them is giving us any indication that they are planning to return to Pennsylvania. I'm sure that, as a mature and responsible parent, I'm supposed to tell my daughters, "It really doesn't matter where you live, as long as you're happy." In my opinion, that's a line of bullshit. The truth of the matter is that my wife and I miss our children and want to remain close to them and *their* children for as long as possible. I have this fantasy that we all come together each and every Sunday for a nice home cooked meal. If you have ever watched the TV series, "Blue Bloods," then you will know what I'm referring to. I guess what I'm really trying to say is that **it does** matter to me where they live. It matters a lot. So why should I lie to them and say that it **doesn't** matter where they live? And what about this crap, "as long as you are happy?" What about **my happiness**? Doesn't that count? Oh wait, in Chapter Three, I said that, as a parent, **it's not about you**. It's about your kids, right? I'm so confused. Once again, I am digressing. Here's my point. I was so upset when I came to the conclusion that my baby girls were never coming home, that I attempted to bribe them. One evening I texted that I would help them with a considerable down payment on a home if they moved back to the Philadelphia area. I never consulted with my wife on this matter and, as you might imagine, she was not a happy camper. In addition, our oldest daughter responded back immediately and berated me. She said that it was totally unethical to "buy her affection" and bribe her into moving back home. Knowing our oldest daughter, I was not the least bit surprised by her comments. She is a moral compass and walks the straight and narrow path in life. Here's the best part. Our middle daughter living in California texted me and said, "Hmmm. Interesting. Make me an offer and then we will talk." Again, different people react differently to this concept of monetary rewards.

Interestingly enough, those that we are attempting to lead in the workplace are no different than the children we are parenting. Some of them will run through a brick wall for monetary rewards and some couldn't care less. I managed salespeople for over two decades and you would think that all salespeople would be 100% motivated by monetary rewards. That has **not** been my personal experience. Some salespeople would track their numbers several times a day to determine their compensation down to the last dollar. They would also take actions which gave them the highest probability of maximizing their compensation. Other salespeople would rarely check their numbers to determine the impact on their compensation. This seems hard to believe since these were professional salespeople.

As a parent and a leader of others, here are a few lessons learned about the role of rewarding others in order to influence their behavior:

Not everyone is motivated to change their behavior based upon monetary rewards

I have had countless arguments with people who are convinced that the **only thing** that truly motivates behavior is monetary rewards. My experiences have not shown this to be the case with either my children or direct reports.

Sometimes rewards can have very negative, unintended consequences

As an example, rewarding others in public can make the recipient of the reward embarrassed. It can also cause others around them to become jealous or resentful.

One of the most powerful tools to influence other's behavior is not *through rewards, but through recognition*

Recognition is an "acknowledgement of achievement, service or merit." Therefore, by definition, unlike Rewards, Recognition has no monetary value. Interestingly enough, providing others with positive recognition or *"catching others doing things right"* is incredibly powerful stuff. I've encountered a lot of people in my life who had lukewarm reactions to receiving monetary rewards. On the other hand, I have seen magic in others who were *"caught doing things right."* That is the secret sauce which I'd like to discuss further.

Catching Others Doing Things Right

I don't know who coined this phrase, but it is priceless. In my opinion, it is truly a best practice for every parent and leader. The beauty of catching others doing things right is that it doesn't cost a dime but the return on investment is remarkable. In my experience, there are two types of people in this world. One type actively catches others doing things right. In other words, they have early detection radar which monitors situations where others around them have done something good, and then they quickly point it out to them. Then there are those who have early detection radar which catches others doing things wrong.

For over 20 years my wife was a stay at home Mom raising three girls. I remember coming home from work and observing my wife's interactions with our daughters. My wife would say, "Carly, you can't eat in the living room. Emily, you didn't put your dish in the sink. Kate, I don't like your tone of voice." Then she would turn to me and say, "You didn't put the garbage can out by the curb this morning." Then I would get defensive and say, "I just walked in the door. How about a simple, 'Hello, how was your day,' as a starter?" In my wife's defense, it is not easy dealing with three daughters 24/7. Make no mistake about that. There are also plenty of opportunities to catch your kids doing things wrong. I get it. One day I asked my wife, "Colleen, was there *anything* that our girls actually did *right* today?" I remember her saying, "Actually, no, nothing comes to mind." This is too funny. I will go on record by saying that, in my opinion, being a stay at home spouse, particularly with three daughters, is far more stressful, challenging and exhausting than any profession I can think of.

In my experience as a parent and a leader of others, there have been three keys to catching others doing things right:

Be Timely

What good does it do to acknowledge someone for doing

something right, nine months after they did something right? What's important is to constantly be on the lookout for really good actions and behaviors in others and then immediately tell them about it.

Be Specific

Speaking in vague generalities is not very effective. Telling someone, "You are doing a great job. Keep up the good work," is pretty close to meaningless, in my opinion. The recipient of this feedback will be left wondering exactly what was meant. Keep up the good work? Exactly what work are we referring to that is so good?

Be Genuine

Whether we realize it or not, when we recognize our children or direct reports, they are not only paying attention to **what** we say, but **how** we say it. I remember an incident which took place in my early years while working for Mobil Chemical. Back in the late 1980s, Mobil offered stock options to talented employees. The intention was to motivate and retain these employees. I was one of the recipients of stock options and I will never forget how they were presented to me. I was sitting at my desk and the phone rang. I answered the phone and the Vice President of Human Resources was on the other line. He said something like this: "Steve, you have been identified as a high potential employee and the company is rewarding you with stock options. You will be receiving further details in the mail. Thanks. Goodbye." It was the coldest, most fabricated message I ever received. It sounded as though the VP wasn't personally in favor of granting me stock options and he couldn't wait to get me off the phone. This was a guy who was not very likeable to begin with. He showed no empathy for others. He was certainly not a "people person." Do you find this ironic: a VP of Human Resources that is not good with people? Sort of like a VP of Accounting that is not good with numbers. Don't get me wrong, I didn't turn down the stock options, but I would have liked to have been shown a little love. Am I wrong in feeling this way? The irony is that soon after receiving the stock options, I left the company anyway. I can't help but feel that if the VP of Human Resources had just given me positive, specific heart felt recognition that I might have stayed with the company for a longer period of time.

I cannot emphasize enough, the power of catching others doing things right and the extent to which this practice can influence the actions and behaviors of others

The impact of providing others with meaningful recognition can never be underestimated. Here are just a few examples of what receiving positive feedback will do for your children and direct reports in the workplace:

It Builds Self Confidence

Has anyone important in your life ever given you positive, genuine recognition for a job well done? If so, do you remember how it made you feel, particularly if you trusted and respected the person recognizing you? I have witnessed, first-hand, the reactions from my children and direct reports at work when they have been recognized for their efforts and accomplishments. They were beaming with pride! Interestingly enough, I think that the positive recognition not only made them more confident in accomplishing the task they were recognized for but made them more confident in themselves in general. That can't be a bad thing, can it?

It Reinforces Their Strengths

I think a lot of people spend a disproportionate amount of time focusing on their weaknesses and how to compensate for them. At the same time, a lot us pay much less attention to our strengths. In many cases, we aren't even aware of what our strengths are. The beauty in catching others doing things right is making them aware of their strengths. As a parent or leader providing positive feedback, it also represents an opportunity to set expectations with children and direct reports. These expectations serve as a reminder to others regarding what **you** *think is noteworthy and important in their actions and behaviors.*

It Leads to Repetition of the Actions and Behaviors Being Recognized

As parents and leaders, when we catch others doing things right, there is a strong likelihood that they will form a habit of repeating the things they have done right. Isn't that what we want?

In summary, rewards and recognition, when applied appropriately and thoughtfully, can be extremely powerful tools to influence other's behaviors. Rewards can be a little tricky because not everyone is motivated to alter their behavior based upon money or monetary equivalents. It can also be very expensive with a low return on investment. Providing recognition, on the other hand, particularly if it is timely, specific and genuine can have a tremendous impact on shaping the behavior of your children and direct reports. It certainly has been the case from my personal experience.

Summary

According to the Bureau of Labor Statistics, there are approximately 24 million managers and front-line supervisors in the United States. There are also 175 million parents who direct, support and care for over two hundred million children. That's an awful lot of people with a tremendous amount of responsibility for influencing the lives of so many others.

Here's the scary part. Given the magnitude of importance of parenting and leading, there is no formal certification process or educational requirements to ensure that parents and leaders are actually *qualified* for these roles. I have no doubt that if a formalized certification process was instituted, a lot of parents and managers would not make the cut. According to one recent management study, over 50% of employees surveyed, quit their jobs because of their manager's failure to effectively lead. It wouldn't surprise me if a few million children would fire their own parents, if they could, for negligence and incompetence.

I believe that parenting and leading others in the workplace is an honor and a privilege. Tragically, there are a lot of parents and workforce leaders who do not share this belief. If I had a nickel for every story I have heard through the years about terrible parenting or leadership, I'd be a wealthy man.

That being said, there are countless parents and workforce leaders that really do get it. They certainly are not perfect, by any means, but their hearts are in the right place. Parenting and leading is a continuous, humbling journey filled with many hazards and detours along the way. Hopefully we learn from our mistakes, get back in the saddle and become a little wiser in the process. The good news is that if our intentions are good, our children and direct reports will cut us some slack. Better yet, they may model our well-intentioned actions and behaviors and "pay it forward" someday with their own children and direct reports.

As a parent and a workforce leader, take the time to realize that your everyday actions are driven by very powerful and deeply rooted underlying values, traits and beliefs. Capitalize on other's strengths, as opposed to correcting their weaknesses. Remember that it's not about you. It's about your kids and direct reports. Keep in mind that our children and direct reports will always pay closer attention to what we do and not what we say. In this day of skyping, zooming, texting and emailing, nothing takes the place of belly to belly, constructive dialogue. The cornerstones of constructive dialogue are to listen intently and ask good, open ended questions. Try to see the big picture and not get completely caught up in too much detail. Coach others to help them become more knowledgeable, skillful, self-confident and independent. Help them to hold themselves accountable for their own actions. Use rewards and recognition to influence the behavior of others. And remember that one of the most powerful recognition tools is to catch others doing things right. If you are a happily married man and you want to remain happily married for the rest of your life, comply with your spouse's wishes and demands. Don't take yourself too seriously. Find a little humor in everything around you. Most importantly, remain humble. Finally, pray for the New York Giants to win another Super Bowl.